MORE
WALK STRAIGHT THROUGH
THE SQUARE

MORE
WALK STRAIGHT THROUGH
THE SQUARE

More
Walk Straight Through
the Square

Walking tours of Europe's most picturesque
cities and towns

Juliann V. Skurdenis &
Lawrence J. Smircich

Maps by
Don Pitcher

David McKay Company, Inc.

New York

To Schwartz, Maximilian, Fritzl, and Ambrose

COPYRIGHT © 1977 BY JULIANN SKURDENIS AND LAWRENCE SMIRCICH

Library of Congress Cataloging in Publication Data

Skurdenis, Juliann V.   1942-
More Walk straight through the square.

Includes index.
1. Europe—Description and travel—1971-   —Tours.
I. Smircich, Lawrence J., 1942-   joint author.
II. Title.   III. Title: Walk straight through the square.
D909.S542   914   76-44359
ISBN 0-679-50644-6
ISBN 0-679-50687-X pbk.

10 9 8 7 6 5 4 3 2 1

MANUFACTURED IN THE UNITED STATES OF AMERICA

Acknowledgments

We wish to express our appreciation and gratitude to Don Pitcher for his preparation of the maps that accompany each of these walking tours; to Donald E. McCormick for his helpful criticism and suggestions; to Patricia Glass Schuman for her unfailing good advice; to Blanche Signorile, our travel agent, for her help in "getting us there"; to Birute L. Skurdenis for her assistance in translating French; and to Catherine Wanger for her help in translating German but especially for her careful scrutiny of this text prior to publication.

CONTENTS

CONTENTS

INTRODUCTION

Over the years, in the course of many trips to Europe, we have developed a "philosophy" of travel. It's a very simple philosophy with one principal tenet—walk! Walking is the only way to get the "feel" of a city, to really experience all it has to offer. This is especially true of European cities—Europe's cities, large and small, have medieval quarters with narrow, winding streets which barely allow automobiles to pass through, much less tour busses. Then too there are the numerous small squares, the parks tucked off in quiet corners of the city, and the pedestrian-only shopping streets, which are either inaccessible or closed to vehicles (except, of course, for bicycles). If you tour Europe by bus, you see its busiest thoroughfares; if you tour on foot, you see not only these thoroughfares but all the lovely, picturesque corners in between which make a trip to Europe so fascinating. Enough said—walk!

Rambling aimlessly through Europe's cities and towns can be fun but few of us have the limitless time that this requires if we want to take in all of a town's important sights. Most of us are on a limited time schedule and our time in Europe is precious. We want to see the well-known sights as well as get the feel of a particular city. So what we have tried to do in our walking tours is to provide a manageable itinerary which takes the walker to almost all the important sights of a city while still giving him a feel for the city's uniqueness by a ramble through its squares, back streets, parks, and marketplaces.

Equally important is the fact that *you* set the pace. Although these walking tours were designed to be completed in one or two days, *you* decide how much or how little you want to see in a given city. If history intrigues you, linger among the tombs and monuments of early English kings and prelates in Winchester Cathedral. If you wander into a market square in Utrecht with a lively flower market in progress, browse a while. If, on the other hand, you've seen all the churches and market squares you care to see on one day, you're free to go on to the next sight or find the nearest pastry shop to reward yourself for all the sightseeing you've been doing (besides, you'll walk off those extra calories in no time!). Imagine trying either to linger a bit longer or to skip a sight which doesn't interest you on a tour bus schedule!

The cities we've included are not the large, often crowded, cities but the smaller, more manageable ones. Most important, they are more typically European than the bustling metropolises most tourists visit. By all means, see London, but Warwick—only a few hours' train or car ride away—with its medieval castle and Elizabethan almshouse is more typically English than cosmopolitan London. Visit Madrid but don't miss Avila—a walk along its narrow streets and beside its ancient walls will transport you back to the Middle Ages. Heidelberg, with its world-famous student inns and ruined castle perched above the town, captures the "heart" of Germany, more so than sophisticated Munich.

The cities we've included are typical of their countries and yet they're also unique: Seville's Alhambra recalls the grandeur of Moorish Spain. Exeter's picturesque coffee houses and taverns take you back to the days of the Elizabethan sea-adventurers, Sir Francis Drake and Sir Walter Raleigh. Delft is the home of a factory where "Delft blue" china is made the same way it was made 300 years ago. Ghent has a unique series of medieval and Renaissance guildhouses. Durham, William the Conqueror's northernmost stronghold, has England's most beautifully situated cathedral. And on and on.

This combination of the typical and the unique to be experienced in the twelve cities chosen here should not be missed, even by the first-time traveler to Europe. Each is easily accessible by car, train, or bus (or in the case of Seville, by plane) from a capital city or other large European metropolis. It is possible to group the cities and visit them one after the other (we've done it).

Besides developing our own philosophy of travel, we've also gathered a litany of hints, cautions, and words of advice to pass on to the walker. Here are a few of them. While it is up to you to determine the pace of the walking tours, we have designed each of the tours to be completed in one day (or, in the case of several of the cities, in two days). We've also designed the walks to begin in the morning in order to take maximum advantage of daylight and of the hours most major sights are open. A word about opening hours for places of interest—they are current as of the writing of these tours. Of course, hours are especially subject to change but will probably vary little from the hours listed in our tours. If at all possible, try to review in advance the walking tours you intend to take so you can plan to be at the various sights when they are open (sometimes in Spain, for example, scheduling requires a bit of juggling because of long lunch hours).

As for shoes (of foremost importance, of course), we have found that comfortable, low-heeled, closed shoes with thick crepe rubber soles are best. They provide a good grip and cushion the omnipresent cobblestones. Also, in rainy weather, closed shoes, with the bit of added height supplied by the crepe soles, are an advantage in keeping feet dry.

The maps which accompany each walking tour trace the route to be followed; all important streets and outstanding sights are labeled. However, it is impossible to label every street, and walkers may wish to pick up an additional, more detailed city map. They are available at low cost from most stationers or tobacconists or free from hotels and local tourist offices. They are not necessary for these walking tours but are nice to have should you want to do additional exploring on your own. We have also included a floor plan and wall elevation diagram of a typical Gothic cathedral which we hope you will find useful.

One final caution: Man is a creature of change. While all the cities in this book are ancient and are unlikely to change a great deal, old buildings come down and new ones go up every day. We have been as accurate as possible. But if, as you walk along, you find that a mansion we pointed out is no longer open or a baptismal font which we say should be in the nave of the church is now in the apse or a lovely little park which once contained a duck pond now contains a parking lot (we hope not many such changes have occurred!), please let us know about it. We've included a short form at the back of the book for you to return to us. We'd appreciate hearing from you.

We loved daydreaming, planning, traveling, and writing this book. We loved walking through Europe's cities. We hope that you too will enjoy these walks through a dozen of Europe's most beautiful cities and towns and that you will be as convinced as we are that walking is the only way to see Europe. It's healthy; you can set your own pace; and it's a bargain! Whether you come to Europe with your personal maid and ten suitcases or with your backpack, we'll show you the best of Europe at about seventy-five cents a city.

If we've convinced you that walking is the only way to go, you'll be glad to know that we've written another book, *Walk Straight Through the Square* (David McKay), which contains walking tours of twelve cities in Austria, France, Italy, Switzerland, and Yugoslavia.

Bon Voyage!

J.V.S.
L.J.S.

New York City
October 1976

MORE
WALK STRAIGHT THROUGH
THE SQUARE

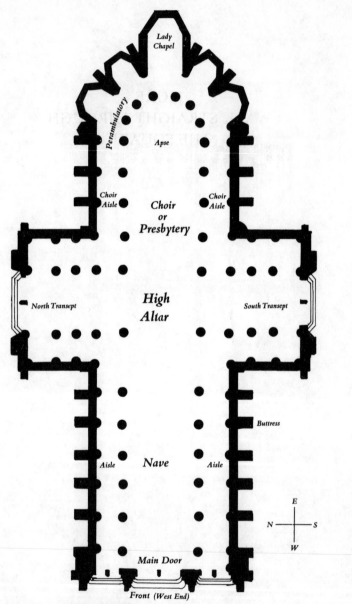

Typical Cathedral Floor Plan

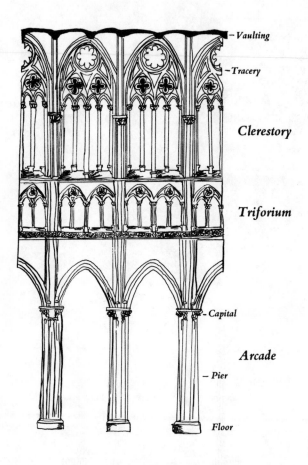

— Vaulting

— Tracery

Clerestory

Triforium

— Capital

Arcade

— Pier

Floor

Typical Cathedral Wall Elevations

BELGIUM

BELGIUM

GHENT

Ghent is the jewel of eastern Flanders, a magnificent city rich in man-made treasures. Its superb spires pierce the Flemish sky; its ornate guildhouses lining the quays testify to the vitality of life here during the Middle Ages; its lovely abbeys, once the centers of the city's spiritual life, now house the accumulated treasures of days gone by. Strolling through this beautiful city, one would never believe that, over the centuries, Ghent has stood in the midst of strife and turbulence. This has never been a city to take a back seat during times of trouble and change. Much of this is because Ghent is part of Flanders, a traditional battleground. But, more important, Ghent has always had the reputation for independence, a desire to determine its own fate.

Ghent began with the foundation of two abbeys by St. Amand in the 7th century and with the settlement which quickly grew up around them. By the 9th century, a fortress-castle had been built and a village sprang up alongside the two rivers which meet here. During the 12th and 13th centuries, Ghent grew to become the most important town in Flanders with an extensive and prosperous cloth-weaving industry. As business grew, so did the power of the wealthy burghers, who wanted to secure certain rights for themselves and their guilds. The clash came in the 14th century between the aristocracy, the vassals of a French king, and the burghers, who craved more independence. In 1302, Jan Borluut led his fellow citizens against French forces; in the 1340s, Jacob van Artevelde allied himself with the English king and led an army against the Count of Flanders; in 1382, van Artevelde's son, Philip, led another army against the king of France.

The 15th century ushered in the return of peace to Flanders and a flowering of the arts. But it was only temporary: Charles V inherited Ghent and Flanders as part of a vast empire which included Spain, Burgundy, and Austria. When the city refused to be taxed in 1540, he marched in, destroying the city's defenses and abolishing its privileges as well. Barely thirty years later,

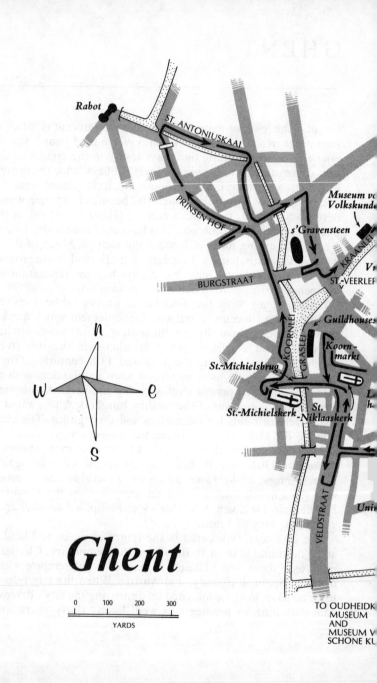

Rabot

ST. ANTONIUSKAAI

PRINSEN HOF

s'Gravensteen

Museum voor
Volkskunde

KRAANLEI

Vr

ST.-VEERLEP

BURGSTRAAT

Guildhouses

KOORNLEI

GRASLEI

Koorn-
markt

St.-Michielsbrug

L

h

St.-Michielskerk

St.
Niklaaskerk

VELDSTRAAT

Uni

Ghent

| 0 | 100 | 200 | 300 |

YARDS

TO OUDHEIDK
MUSEUM
AND
MUSEUM V
SCHONE KU

n

w — e

s

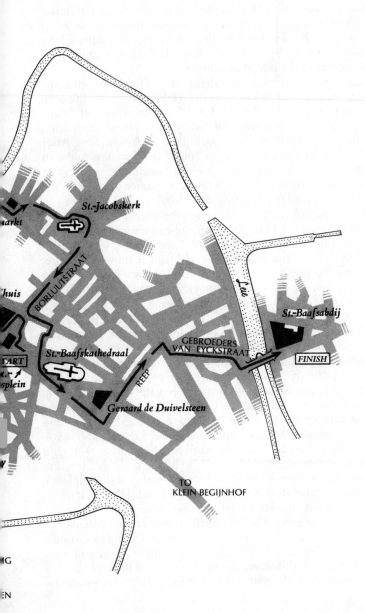

St.-Jacobskerk

aarkt

BORLUUTSTRAAT

huis

START

splein

St.-Baafskathedraal

REEP

Geraard de Duivelsteen

GEBROEDERS
VAN EYCKSTRAAT

Leie

St.-Baafsabdij

FINISH

TO
KLEIN BEGIJNHOF

NG

EN

Charles V's son, Philip II, disturbed by the growth of Calvinism in the Low Countries, sent his general, the notorious Duke of Alba, to quell this trend toward Protestantism. Alba initiated the Inquisition and the Spanish-style autos-da-fé. The Spanish were finally ousted in the late 16th century.

Again quiet returned to Ghent and Flanders, until the invasion of the French early in the 18th century, an invasion which was reversed by John Churchill, the Duke of Marlborough, and Prince Eugene of Savoy. A hundred years later, Napoleon was routed at Waterloo, not too far from Ghent. After another hundred years, Flanders found itself in the midst of World War I; the Germans occupied Belgium, and again repeated the outrage in World War II. But, once again as in the past, Ghent, Flanders, and Belgium recovered.

Ghent has miraculously survived the ravages of wars and time. It has mellowed into the beautiful city we will enjoy today. The one walking tour suggested will keep you busy for a long, very full day, so you might want to break it into two smaller segments. Whatever you decide, take your time strolling along the quays, visiting the former abbeys, and browsing through the flea market of this queen of Belgian cities.

Begin your walk through Ghent at one of its most impressive monuments, **St.-Baafskathedraal** (Cathedral of St. Bavo). Located in St.-Baafsplein, in the heart of the city, this church is one of the most splendid in Belgium. Its construction and decoration span eight centuries; there's hardly a trace left of the building which was begun in the 10th century, but the crypt dates from the middle of the 12th century and is the oldest part of the present cathedral. The choir was added in the 14th and 15th centuries, and the 280-foot Gothic bell tower looming above you (which you can ascend between April and September, 9–12 and 2–6) was built between 1462 and 1538. By the middle of the 16th century, the exterior of the church as it is today was completed. The interior decoration was finished two hundred years later, in the 18th century, the era of baroque extravagance.

Enter the cathedral (hours: April to September, Monday to Saturday, 7–12, 2–6:30; Sunday, 12:45–6:30; October to March, Monday to Saturday, 7–12, 2:30–4:30; Sunday, 2–5) and walk down the late Gothic nave, the final portion of the church to be built. Along the walls notice the paintings, which are mostly by

17th-century Belgians. The baroque oak **pulpit** with the colossal marble figures dates from the mid-18th century and was carved by Laurent Delvaux, one of the foremost sculptors of the era.

Proceed to the south transept, from which you enter the ambulatory encircling the east end of the cathedral. The first chapel you pass contains a **masterpiece of Frans Pourbus the Elder** painted in 1571; it represents the boy Jesus expounding on the Scriptures, surrounded by the elders of the temple. The painting is especially interesting because it includes, in the left foreground, the portraits of Charles V, the Holy Roman Emperor, Philip II of Spain, Charles's son and heir, and Fernando Alvarez de Toledo, the Duke of Alba.

Enter the choir from the ambulatory, noting the beautiful black-and-white marble screens, the gift of the 17th-century bishop, Antonie Triest. Bishop Triest rests on the north side of this choir, in the company of three other of Ghent's bishops. The red bronze candlesticks in front of the altar were originally intended to be pillars for the tomb of England's Henry VIII and bear his coat of arms; Oliver Cromwell sold them in the middle of the 17th century, during his devastation of English churches, and they were purchased by Bishop Triest, who turned them into candlesticks. Above the altar is a statue of the cathedral's patron saint, St. Bavo, ascending to heaven.

Walk now to the sixth chapel in the ambulatory, to see one of the most perfect medieval altarpieces in existence and the masterpiece of the early Flemish school of art, the polyptych called the **Adoration of the Lamb** (hours: Easter to September, Monday to Saturday, 9:30–12, 2–6; Sunday, 1–6; October to Easter, Monday to Saturday, 10:30–12, 2:30–4; Sunday, 2–5). The altarpiece was painted between 1420 and 1432 by Hubert and Jan van Eyck for the Ghent patrician Joos Vydt. The van Eyck brothers, natives of the town of Masseyck near Maastricht, spent a number of years painting in Ghent. Hubert, the older of the brothers, never lived to see the painting completed; he died here in Ghent in 1426. Jan completed the painting six years after Hubert's death; he died in Bruges in 1441.

The *Adoration* altarpiece is large: twelve feet high and fifteen feet wide when the side panels are open. The painting consists of twelve panels of varying sizes symbolically representing the central events in the story of man's fall and redemption. On the top extreme left and right are Adam and Eve, mankind's original parents, who lost the earthly paradise into which they had been placed. Above their heads are their children, Cain and Abel: above Adam, Abel offering a sacrifice to God with Cain jealously watching; above Eve, Abel being slain by Cain. The central event of the painting is represented in the bottom center panel: Here the sacrificial lamb, symbol of the crucified Christ, stands atop an altar surrounded by adoring angels. He represents man's salvation and redemption from the original sin of Adam and Eve. To the left of the lamb, set against a background rich in natural beauty—trees and flowers—and man-made beauty—church spires—is a procession of bishops; to the right is a procession of virgins. In the foreground, on either side of the fountain of life, are patriarchs and prophets on the left, representatives of the Old Testament, and Apostles and confessors on the right, representatives of the New Testament. The panel to the left of this center panel shows knights on horseback and, in the adjacent panel the just judges. Hubert and Jan included themselves among the judges: Hubert has long brown hair, wears a fur hat and a fur-lined mantle, and rides a white horse. Jan, looking toward his brother, is dressed in brown, wears a turban, and rides a brown horse. The panels to the right of the center panel present hermits and pilgrims led by a gigantic St. Christopher. Above the center panel is Christ in majesty between the blessed Virgin and John the Baptist. Between them and Adam and Eve are more angels. On the reverse side of these panels appears an Annunciation scene, and below it are portraits of the donor, Joos Vydt, and his wife, Isabelle Borluut. Between them are John the Baptist and John the Evangelist. This altarpiece, the superlative example of the early Flemish school of painting, is a masterwork of rich detail: Notice the landscape, with the evidence of a bustling Belgian town just beyond. Also carefully note the angels, hermits, virgins, and knights. This is not just a conglomeration of faces— each one is a unique portrait.

The *Adoration* altarpiece has had a turbulent 550-year history. It escaped the destruction of the Puritans in 1566 and the ravages of fire in 1640 and in 1832. But in 1794 the French took it to Paris to hang in the Louvre. When it was restored to Ghent 22 years later, portions of it had been sold to the Berlin

Museum. Finally, in 1920, in accordance with the terms of the Treaty of Versailles ending World War I, the missing panels were restored. But, 14 years later, one of the lower panels—that of the just judges—was stolen, and has not been located to this day. During World War II the painting was hidden in southern France, but it was discovered in 1942 and transported to Germany by the Nazis. After the war, it was once again returned to the Cathedral of St. Bavo.

Continue along the ambulatory to the tenth chapel, where you can see another magnificent altarpiece, this one painted by **Peter Paul Rubens** in 1624 and representing St. Bavo entering the abbey of St. Amand in Ghent. Bavo was born in the Brabant (the area around Brussels) sometime in the late 6th or early 7th century. He became a wealthy landowner, married, and had one daughter, but led a licentious life. After his wife's death, however, he "saw the light," abandoned his previous ways, distributed his possessions among the poor (which you see his steward doing in the lower portion of the painting), and became a missionary accompanying another Belgian saint, Amand, throughout France and Flanders. His final years were spent living as a hermit in the woods near Ghent. Rubens painted himself as St. Bavo kneeling at the abbey entrance.

Now visit the north transept, to see the **triptych of the Crucifixion** painted by Justus van Gent in the late 15th century. Also in this transept are fourteen paintings depicting incidents from the life of St. Andrew painted in the middle of the 16th century by Frans Pourbus the Elder. From the north transept visit the **crypt,** which also houses the **treasury** (hours: April to September, Monday to Saturday, 9:30–12, 2–6; Sunday, 1–6; closed October to March). The crypt, the oldest portion of the present cathedral, is decorated with 15th–16th century murals and is the final resting place of many of Ghent's bishops. You can see illuminated manuscripts as well as ornate reliquaries (note the reliquary in the shape of John the Baptist's head).

As you leave the cathedral, stop by the second chapel from the north transept, dedicated to St. Macharius. It's richly decorated in 19th-century neo-Gothic style.

Return to St.-Baafsplein and walk toward the belfry directly in front of you. You pass the monument to Jan Frans Willems, 19th-century poet, playwright, and philologist, who was a leader and exponent of Flemish nationalism. Across from him, to your right, is the Renaissance-style Royal Flemish Theater. Continue a few steps to the **Belfry.** Rising almost three hundred feet, this solid-looking 14th-century bell tower crowned with five spires contains a carillon of fifty-two bells. Thirty-seven of these bells were cast in 1660 by Peter Hemony of Amsterdam, one of the foremost bell casters of the age. Surmounting the tower is a 14th-century brass dragon, supposedly brought from Constantinople to Bruges during the Fourth Crusade. No one knows how it got from Bruges to Ghent.

You can ascend the tower for a stupendous view over the city from the adjacent **Lakenhalle** (Cloth Hall). Built in the second quarter of the 15th century, this hall was used as a warehouse, market, and meetingplace by the town's wool merchants. Today you can view an interesting 20-minute "audio-visual play" about Holy Roman Emperor Charles V (hours: April to September, 8:30–11:30, 1:00–5:30; October to March, 8:30–11:30, 1:00–3:30; performances are continuous). Charles, the son of Philip the Fair and Joanna the Mad and grandson of Ferdinand and Isabella of Spain (Joanna's parents) and Maximilian of Austria and Mary of Burgundy (Philip's parents), was born in the Prinsenhof here in Ghent in February of 1500. He was heir to the huge Spanish-Austrian-Burgundian empire, not to mention the lands in the newly discovered American continent. And, in 1519, when only nineteen years old, he was elected Holy Roman Emperor. Although he had an affection for Ghent, his birthplace, when the townspeople refused to finance his military expeditions, he himself marched on the town in 1540 to destroy its defense system and build a new fortress. In the vaulted undercroft of the Lakenhalle is a restaurant, the Raadskelder, to which you might want to return later for lunch or dinner.

From the Lakenhalle, walk around the building into Ghent's ancient Botermarkt (Butter Market). On the northeast corner of Botermarkt is St.-Jorishof (St. George's Court), a stern fortresslike structure which claims to be the oldest hotel in Europe, having served travelers since 1228. Opposite the hotel is Ghent's **Stadhuis** (Town Hall). Begun in 1518 on the site of an earlier 14th-century town hall, the building was intended to rival the impressive town halls in the cities of Brussels and Louvain. But in 1540, with only the ornate Gothic north façade completed, the town lost its privileges because of its resistance to Charles V's taxation, and construction halted. It was not resumed again until the late 16th–early 17th centuries, when the Renaissance-style east façade was finished. Religious conflicts intervened this time, and the remaining two façades were not completed until the 18th century. You can enter the Stadhuis (hours: April to September, Monday to Saturday, 9–11:30, 2–4:30; Sunday, 9–11:30; October to March, Monday to Saturday, 9–11:30, 2–3:30; closed Sunday) to visit some of its splendid rooms. On the ground floor, see the grand Pacificatiezaal (Pacification Hall), where the Pacification of Ghent was signed in 1576 by the seventeen states comprising the Low Countries. This treaty expelled the Spanish from the Low Countries, named William of Orange (leader of the resistance against the Spanish) stadholder, or prince of Holland, and guaranteed religious toleration throughout the Low Countries. Visit also the Trouwzaal (Marriage Hall), which was once a chapel; here hangs a canvas depicting Charles V's grandmother, Mary of Burgundy, interceding for the lives of two of her ministers accused of treason. On the upper floor, reached via a fine Gothic staircase, visit the Troonzaal (Throne Room), a huge Gothic hall hung with canvases depicting important events in the history of the Low Countries: See the Abdication of Charles V by Gaspard de Crayer and the statues of Charles V and his two sets of grandparents. Nearby is the Collatiezaal (Banqueting Hall), with its lovely 15th-century timbered ceiling and chimneypieces.

From the Stadhuis return to the belfry. Just to the left of the tower in Burgemeester Braunplein is a fountain with kneeling figures and, close by, the great Triomfante, one of the bells cast by Peter Hemony, which hung in the belfry from 1660 until 1914, when it cracked. Directly in front of you is the east end of St.-Niklaaskerk. Skirt the north side of the church, along the street called Klein Turkije (Little Turkey). Nestled against the side of the church is a row of quaint little cottages, and across the street is an ancient inn called **Rode Hoed** (Red Hat), where Albrecht Dürer lodged on his visit to Ghent in 1521. For several centuries before it became an inn, the Rode Hoed housed the Grocer's Guild. At the end of Klein Turkije, turn right into Koornmarkt (Corn Market). On the right side of this wide street, at Nos. 6–7, is **Borluutsteen,** the medieval mansion of one of

Ghent's leading families, the Borluuts. In 1302, Jan Borluut led the townspeople against the superior forces of the French king in an attempt to protect the city's rights and privileges. Isabelle Borluut was the wife of Joos Vydt, the patron of the Adoration altarpiece. On both sides of this street are Renaissance houses.

Return to St.-Niklaaskerk (St. Nicholas's Church), whose bell tower, together with the belfry and the cathedral's bell tower, completes the triumvirate of magnificent towers piercing Ghent's skyline. Parts of the church (the base of the tower, the west doorway) date from the early 13th century, and this bulky-looking edifice with its numerous arcaded turrets is a good example of medieval Flemish architecture. The church is temporarily closed. Inside it is a pillar with an inscription recording the burial place of Oliver van Minjau. Oliver and his wife set a near world's record by having thirty-one children. The entire family died in 1526 during a plague epidemic.

Walk past St.-Niklaaskerk into Veldstraat (Field Street). At the corner of Veldstraat and Volderstraat, on the left, is the **Lovendegham mansion,** disfigured by a storefront on the ground level. This mansion was the residence of the American representatives during the negotiations in 1814 which culminated in the Treaty of Ghent. For five months, Henry Clay and John Quincy Adams (later to become sixth president of the United States) worked on the treaty which ended the War of 1812 between Great Britain and the United States and guaranteed freedom of the seas to the former colony. Practically next door, at No. 55, is the 18th-century **Hotel d'Hane-Steenhuyse,** which served as the residence of Louis XVIII during the "100 days" in 1815 when Napoleon made his comeback from exile on the island of Elba. Czar Alexander I was also once a guest here. Finally, cross the street to No. 82, the former Vander Haeghen mansion.

Now make a short detour to the right along Volderstraat to see Ghent's University, founded in 1816 by King William I. Since 1930, the courses have been given entirely in Flemish, a variant of Dutch. Although French is the official language of Belgium, the Flemish are proud of their own language and insisted that it be used in their university.

Return toward the front of St.-Niklaaskerk and turn left to St.-Michielsbrug (St. Michael's Bridge). From this bridge you have a panorama of some of the most impressive and famous sights in Ghent: directly ahead the trio of towers of St.-Niklaaskerk, the belfry, and St.-Baafskathedraal. To the left as you face St.-Niklaaskerk stands the massive feudal fortress s'Gravensteen, almost hidden by other buildings. Also to your left is Ghent's most famous array of houses, the quaint gabled guildhouses along the **Graslei** (Herb Quay). Wait until you're walking along the quay opposite the Graslei for a better view of these charming buildings. You must return to the St.-Michielsbrug at night, when all these buildings and bell towers are floodlit—the scene is truly spectacular! Continue across the bridge to **St.-Michielskerk,** with its incomplete, stunted bell tower. This church, finally completed in the middle of the 17th century after two centuries of building, is one of the last churches to be built in the heart of the city.

Return to the bridge and take the steps down to the **Koornlei** (Grain Quay), lined with many lovely 17th- and 18th-century houses. From this quay you have the best view of the guild-houses along the Graslei across the river. To start, the building which is easiest to identify is the plain gray Romanesque building, called the **Stapelhuis** or Spijker. Built about the year 1200, it has served over the centuries as a granary. To its right is the tiny customs house called the **Tolhuisje** (Toll House), built in 1682. Next door is the graceful **Gildehuis der Graanmeters** (Guildhouse of the Grain Measurers), dating from 1698. Finally, the building crowned with the fanciful gables is the **Gildehuis der Vrije Schippers** (Guildhouse of the Free Boatmen). Considered the finest guildhouse in Belgium, this Gothic structure was completed in 1531 for the men who loaded and unloaded cargo. Membership in this guild brought power and privileges (these men controlled all shipping on the river), and it was passed from father to son in the manner of an inheritance.

Returning now to the Stapelhuis: To its left stands the 15th-century **Korenmeterhuis** (Grain Measurers' House), and to its left is the elegant light-colored stone building with a high, pinnacled façade, the **Gildehuis van de Metsers** (Guildhouse of the Masons), built in 1526. This fantastic row of buildings spans five centuries of Flemish architecture.

Continue along Koornlei. The house at No. 7 with the gilded boat way on top was built in 1740 as the guildhouse of the "unfree" boatmen. These men also loaded and unloaded cargo on Ghent's rivers, but they were not as privileged as their fellow boatmen across the river—hence, the term "unfree."

Proceed straight ahead to Jan-Breydelstraat. At No. 7 you come to the fine mid-18th-century mansion called Hotel de Coninck (King), which now houses the **Museum voor Sier-kunsten,** Ghent's Museum of Decorative Arts. Inside (hours: 9–12, 2–5) you can view a lavishly furnished mansion. At the corner of Burgstraat and Gewad is an interesting 16th-century mansion called the Huis der Gekroonde Hoofden, the House of Crowned Heads, because of the portraits of the Counts of Flanders (including Charles V and Philip II) decorating its façade. At the end of Gewad, make a short detour along Abrahamstraat to see the building on the left side of the street at No. 15, with the elegant classical doorway and the words MONS PIETATIS above the door. This is now Ghent's archives, but for three hundred years, between 1622 and 1930, this building housed the public pawn shop.

Return up Abrahamstraat and turn left along Prinsenhof, an unpretentious street which was once the site of a huge castle built in 1353 and occupied by the Counts of Flanders. Charles V was born in this castle in February of 1500. All that's left now is a vaulted archway beneath two turrets, the **Donkere Poort** (Dark Gateway). You can see the two turrets from the other side. A few steps farther beyond the gateway, cross the bridge, from which you see on the left a small gem of a medieval military fortification, the **Rabot,** which Charles V surprisingly left intact when he destroyed Ghent's defense system in 1540.

Turn right along St.-Antoniuskaai past the almshouse at No. 9, which was built in 1532 by the Guild of Arquebusiers (these were the people who handled a weapon called the harquebus, a light handgun). Follow the river until you come to Lievestraat on your left. At the end of Lievestraat, turn right on Geld-muntstraat (Money Street) to reach **St.-Veerleplein,** a pictur-esque square with a pillar topped by a Flemish lion marking the site where executions were carried out from the 15th to the 18th centuries. During the Inquisition conducted by Spanish Catho-lics in the middle of the 16th century, Lutheran heretics were burned at the stake here. In the corner is a doorway leading to the former *vismarkt* (fish market); you can't miss it, because of the statue of Triton towering above.

But the highlight of this square is **s'Gravensteen** (Counts' Castle), one of the most impressive and best-preserved feudal fortresses in Europe. A fortress was built on this site in the 9th century by Baldwin of the Iron Arm, the first count of Flanders, as a stronghold against invading Norsemen. Three centuries later, the present castle took shape under another count of Flanders, Philip of Alsace. During the turbulent 14th century, the citizens of the city stormed the citadel several times. In the centuries that followed, s'Gravensteen was used as a prison, a mint, law courts, and even, during the 19th century, as a cotton mill. It has now been restored to the period of its "golden age," the 14th century. You can guide yourself around the castle (hours: April to September, 9–5:15; October to March, 9–3:15) by obtaining a guidebook and following the numbers indicated on the wall. You will visit the gatehouse, the courtyard, the dungeon, the Great Hall, and a room with an array of torture instruments including a guillotine used until a century ago.

Leave s'Gravensteen and turn left on Kraanlei (Crane Quay), with its Renaissance gabled houses overlooking the river. At No. 63, you come to the **Museum voor Volkskunde** (Folklore Museum), housed in a 14th-century almshouse. Actually, the museum is housed in eighteen charming medieval houses which were once all part of the almshouse. It's a lovely museum (hours: April to October, 9–12, 1:30–5:30; November to March, 10–11:30, 1:30–4:30; closed Tuesday) depicting the style of life in Ghent at the turn of the 19th century. You can visit the chemist, candlemaker, tinsmith, printer, and numerous other tradesmen of yesteryear.

Continue along Kraanlei, noting some of the interesting houses along the way, particularly Nos. 73, 77, and 79. Cross the Zuivelbrug, which leads to Groot Kanonplein (Big Cannon Square), aptly named for the huge cast-iron cannon in the middle. This 16-ton cannon, nicknamed "Dulle Griet" (Mad Meg), was made for Philip the Good of Burgundy in 1452, and fired stone balls weighing 750 pounds. Adjacent to Groot Kanonplein is the huge square called **Vrijdagmarkt** (Friday Market), the scene of a busy market on Friday mornings as well as Saturday afternoons. Vrijdagmarkt has figured prominently in Ghent's history: It was in this square that the counts of Flanders took their oath to maintain the city's ancient privileges.

It was also here, during the Middle Ages, that guilds used to meet—sometimes to fight. In 1345, a riot broke out here between the weavers and the fullers which resulted in many hundred deaths. The Duke of Alba held his autos-da-fé, burning heretics and opponents of Spanish rule, here in this square. Walk to the middle to see the bronze **statue of Jacob van Artevelde,** the wealthy 14th-century cloth merchant who united the cities of Flanders into resistance against the counts. Artevelde allied himself with Edward III of England, an alliance of expediency, since England had the sheep and Flanders the looms and the weavers. Besides, the Flemish counts were the vassals of the French king, and France and England were natural enemies. Artevelde was assassinated in 1345.

The building with the tall slim turret on the corner of the square is **Het Toreken** (Small Tower), and was built in 1480 as the guildhouse of Ghent's tanners. Walk diagonally through the square toward **St.-Jacobskerk** (St. James Church), with its two Romanesque west towers; most of the church, however, belongs to the late Gothic period. North of the church in Beverhoutplein (Beaver Wood Square) is the site of a twice-weekly flea market (Friday, 7–1; Saturday, 7–6).

Walk around the east end of St.-Jacobskerk and stroll directly ahead along Borluutstraat until you come to Hoogpoortstraat (High Gate Street), a street with numerous interesting houses. At Nos. 50 and 52 are two lovely gabled houses called **Grote Moor** (Big Moor) and **Zwarte Moor** (Black Moor). Next door, at No. 54, is another gabled house, **Grote Sikkel,** named after its first owners, the Van der Sickelen family. This mansion is now a music conservatory. Turn right along Biezekapelstraat to visit the turreted **Achter Sikkel** (Behind the Sikkel), a 15th-century manor house with cylindrical towers of varying sizes.

You now can see the cathedral directly in front of you. Walk along the south side of the cathedral, past the tiny park with the monument to Hubert and Jan van Eyck, toward the sturdy-looking gray mass called **Geraard de Duivelsteen** (Castle of Gerard the Devil). This castle, built in the early 13th century, is a survivor of the many fortified manor houses which once dotted the city of Ghent. In the 750 years of its existence, it has served many functions: private residence, arsenal, convent, orphanage, prison, even fire headquarters. In front of the castle is a monument to Lieven Bauwens, Ghent's 19th-century burgomaster who introduced the spinning jenny—the power loom which wove cotton—into Belgium.

From Geraard de Duivelsteen, turn left and stroll up the boulevard called the Reep, which only a few years ago was a canal linking Ghent's two rivers. Turn right and then left on Gebroeders van Eyckstraat and walk to the bridge crossing the Leie. Straight ahead after you've crossed is **St.-Baafsabdij** (St. Bavo's Abbey), the biggest landowner in Flanders during the Middle Ages. St.-Baafs was a Benedictine abbey founded by St. Amand, a French missionary bishop, in the middle of the 7th century. It was destroyed by the Normans in the 9th century and rebuilt by the counts of Flanders in the 10th century. During the 1300s it grew to become one of the most powerful and wealthy abbeys in the Low Countries. John of Gaunt, Duke of Lancaster and the fourth son of Edward III of England and Philippa of Hainault, was born here in 1340 (Gaunt is the Anglicized form of Ghent). John was to become the father of the first of the Lancastrian kings, Henry IV. Here, in 1369, Philip the Bold of Burgundy married Marguerite, heiress of Louis de Male, the last count of Flanders, thus uniting Flanders and the Burgundian empire. In 1540, Charles V, descendent of Philip and Marguerite, demolished much of the abbey in retaliation for the citizens' refusal to finance his military escapades.

Today the ruins of the abbey house a lapidary museum (hours: 9–12, 2–5). You can stroll along the Gothic cloister, visiting the small 12th-century lavatorium and the 13th-century chapter house. The imposing Romanesque refectory now shelters the collection of stones, including the alleged tombstone of Hubert van Eyck and the tomb of John of Cleves and his wife (he was the father of Anne of Cleves, the fourth wife of Henry VIII). Here you conclude your walk through the city.

* * *

There are also three mini-excursions you should try to fit in during your stay in Ghent. All are within the city limits, but each takes you far enough away (about one mile) from the center of the city, St.-Baafsplein, and from the next sight so that a little "excursion" is necessary. You can hire a taxi to go from one place to another, drive yourself, or ask for bus directions. All three sights can be visited in one morning or afternoon.

Start at the **Oudheidkundig Museum** (Museum of Antiquities), on Godshuizenlaan (House of God Street). This museum, housed in a former 13th-century Cistercian abbey, contains one of the richest collections in Belgium, with treasures from all eras of Ghent's history. Enter the museum through the impressive 17th-century doorway (hours: April to September, 10–12:30, 1:30–5:30; from October to March, museum closes one hour earlier). There are a few sights you should definitely see: Room 1, called the Room of the Governors of the Poorhouse, which dates from the 17th century and was once part of the Town Hall; Room 7, the long wooden-vaulted refectory, built in 1325 and decorated with frescoes. Don't miss the marvelous tomb of a 13th-century nobleman. Room 16 contains arms and armor, and the adjoining room displays prehistoric, Roman, and Frankish antiquities. Finally, visit Rooms 20 to 24, which are decorated in the style of the 17th to 19th centuries.

Next stop at the **Museum voor Schone Kunsten** (Museum of Fine Arts), one of Belgium's most important provincial museums. Set on the edge of the lovely, spacious Citadel Park on Hofbouwlaan, the museum (hours: 9–6) houses a good collection of Flemish art from the 15th to the 20th centuries, including a work or two of Jacob Jordaens, Antoon van Dyck, and Pieter Paul Rubens, all 17th-century geniuses. Besides paintings, there are also drawings, sculptures, and engravings.

Finally, see the **Klein Begijnhof**, at 65 Lange Violettenstraat. The Beguines, unique to Belgium, Holland, and parts of Germany, are lay nuns whose origin stretches back to the 7th century and St. Begga. Even though they are not bound by religious vows, each nun observes certain rules. They do charity work, making lace to earn a living, and each nun lives in her own little house. There are few Begijnhofs left in Belgium and Holland, and this one is a particularly good example. Set around a courtyard are the cottages, where the Beguines live and work. They have remained unaltered since the 17th century.

ENGLAND

DURHAM

"Half church of God, half castle 'gainst the Scot"—this is the way Sir Walter Scott saw Durham and its cathedral in the early 19th century. His words succinctly capture the raison d'être of not only Durham's cathedral, but of its castle as well: Both share a sandstone bluff high above the River Wear, a site which is one of the loveliest and most dramatic in England. The cathedral and castle have their origins in the 11th century, when it was still possible (and often necessary) to build structures which could serve the dual purpose of glorification of God and defense against enemies.

Durham Castle owes its beginning to William the Conqueror, who, about the year 1072, recognized the potential of the spectacular bluff and commenced building a castle-fortress at the neck of that bluff. William vested in Durham's first Norman bishop, who already possessed spiritual jurisdiction, civil jurisdiction as well. William very wisely realized several important factors. He himself was busy establishing his rule in southern England, with little time for the northern part of his realm. But the Scots were making numerous marauding raids in northern England. William conveyed the powers of a palatinate—which included levying taxes, summoning parliaments, and calling up armies in exchange for defense of the northern border—but shrewdly vested these civil powers, not in a prince, whose privileges would have become hereditary, but in a prince-bishop, whose privileges came to him not through inheritance but only upon his election to the Durham bishopric. This dual spiritual-civil role continued until 1836. Thus, Durham Castle became the center of civil rule as well as the home of the spiritual leader of Durham.

Durham Cathedral owes its origin to Bishop William of St. Calais, who in 1093 decided to replace the already existing Saxon church with a grander one which would serve as a more appropriate shrine for St. Cuthbert, patron saint of Durham. This cathedral was primarily God's house, a place of worship for

21

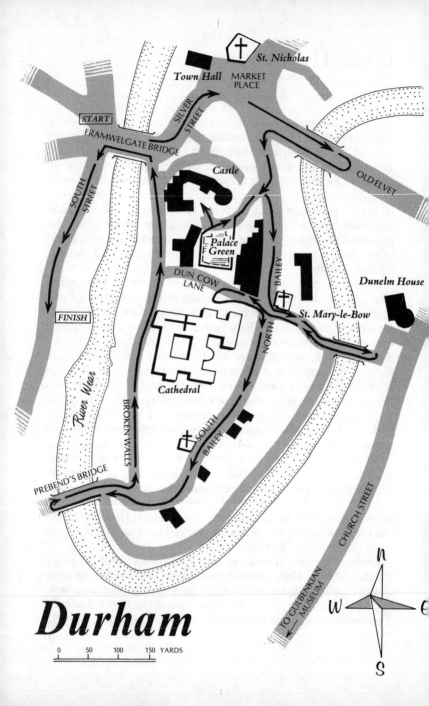

the community, but there always lurked in the background the fact that, if need be, the cathedral could become a second defense for the town and castle.

It is appropriate that cathedral and castle, joint guardians of spiritual and civil power, should stand atop this hundred-foot bluff like two sentinels. Beginning with the end of the 11th century, the town of Durham grew quickly, its houses clustering around the base of the bluff and only gradually spilling over onto the opposite bank of the river.

Today you will walk through the portion of Durham which was the medieval town as well as through the newer Georgian "suburbs" before coming to the two highpoints of Durham, cathedral and castle, which dominate the town. You will end your walk through this magnificent cathedral city with a stroll along the riverside and a final look at the two imposing Norman monuments.

Begin your stroll through Durham on **Framwelgate Bridge,** which crosses the River Wear just beneath the castle. The bridge on which you're standing is 15th-century and was widened in the 19th century. The first bridge to cross the river at this point was constructed in the early 12th century by Durham's prince-bishop, Ranulf Flambard. From this bridge you have a magnificent view of the castle looming above you and the cathedral to its right. To your right, downriver, you can see the weir with the picturesque Prebend's Bridge just beyond.

From Framwelgate Bridge, turn left into **Silver Street,** one of Durham's many picturesque streets, and also one of the town's narrowest. Silver Street leads to the town's triangular **Market Place.** In the middle of the "square" stands the equestrian statue of Charles William Vane Stewart, the third Marquess of Londonderry. Lord Londenderry, who was the half brother of Lord Castlereagh, had a busy and distinguished career in the first half of the 19th century. He was a member of Parliament, undersecretary of war during the administration of his half brother, adjutant general to the Duke of Wellington, and ambassador to Prussia and, later, to Vienna. His statue was erected in 1861, seven years after his death. On the left side of the square is Durham's **Town Hall.** Although the present Town Hall dates only from the middle of the 19th century, Town or

Guild Halls have existed on this site for the past 600 years. Go inside to see the Mayor's Chamber, with its 18th-century wood paneling and remarkable Jacobean fireplace. The fireplace once belonged to Durham's famous coaching inn, the Red Lion, which is now part of Hatfield College. The paintings on the wall are copies of portraits of Charles I and his queen, Henrietta Maria, by Van Dyck. Next door to the Town Hall is the church of St. Nicholas, which has its origins in the 12th century, although the building you see today dates only from 1858. The interior gives an impression of dignified and simple elegance.

If you're fortunate enough to be in Durham on a Saturday, stroll through the colorful covered market just to the left of Town Hall. Leave Market Place at its southeast end and enter Saddler Street, once called Fleshergate, the section of town where the butchers formerly had their shops. Take the left fork, and directly in front of you is **Elvet Bridge,** built by Bishop Hugh du Puiset (who is better known by his Anglicized name, Pudsey) about the year 1160. The great flood of 1771, which wreaked havoc through all of northeastern England, destroyed three arches of Elvet Bridge. It was repaired and widened early in the 19th century. On the far side of the bridge is the suburb of Elvet, which grew and developed during the 18th century. **Old Elvet,** the wide street which begins at the bridge, is still lined with numerous handsome 18th-century Georgian houses. Spend a few minutes strolling along Old Elvet, enjoying its graceful air.

Return to the bridge, cross over, take the first left, and you are once again on **Saddler Street.** Behind the house at No. 61 used to be the late-18th-century theater where Stephen Kemble was manager. Kemble was a member of a famous family of actor-managers: Two of his brothers were actors, as was his sister, Sarah Kemble Siddons. Mrs. Siddons, known in her day as the "queen of the English theater," acted here in the early 19th century. Next to the house, at No. 41, is an alleyway, one of many in Durham, called a vennel. Vennels lead from busy main thoroughfares down to the riverside, and this one, called Drury Lane, gives a view of the river below. At the head of the street once stood the 15th-century North Gate, which was, unfortunately, pulled down in 1820 because it supposedly impeded the flow of traffic.

Just off to the right is **Owen-Gate,** leading to the Palace Green. On your left you pass the almshouses built in 1838 to replace the almshouses originally located on Palace Green, which were taken over by the University in 1836. In a few steps you enter **Palace Green,** the large open space surrounded by buildings representing many eras in Durham's history. Until the 12th century, Palace Green was used as the city's marketplace. But with the completion of the cathedral, Bishop Flambard ordered the market to be removed and it was relocated to its present site north of the castle in Market Place.

Stroll to your left, and the first building you pass is called Bishop Cosin's Hall, in honor of the 17th-century prince-bishop John Cosin. It dates from the Restoration. This building, like most enclosing Palace Green, was incorporated into University College when Durham University was founded, in 1832. Next to Bishop Cosin's Hall are the almshouses built by Bishop Cosin in 1666 to house eight poor men and women of the town; the almshouses in Owen-Gate replaced these 17th-century buildings, which were taken over by the newly founded University. The University lecture rooms are next door. At the end of the row of buildings on this side of Palace Green is Abbey House, which was built during the reign of Queen Anne in the early 18th century.

Dominating the south side of Palace Green is the massive cathedral, which we will visit later on. In the southwest corner is the Old Grammar School, built in 1661, just a year after the restoration of the monarchy. The paneling inside contains the graffiti of generations of Durham's schoolboys.

Proceeding along the west side of Palace Green, you pass an early-19th-century building which stands next to the University Library, built on the site of the former bishop's stables. Beside this library is Bishop Cosin's library, established in 1669 for the use of the local clergy under the bishop's jurisdiction. Next comes the old University Library, housed in the building constructed about 1450 by Bishop Robert Neville as his Exchequer. Note his coat of arms on the façade.

Finally, you come to the **Castle,** one of the high points of a visit to Durham. The castle owes its origin to William the Conqueror, who decided to build a fortress to guard the neck of the peninsula around which the River Wear flows. Because William was kept continuously busy fighting and keeping order in the southern part of England, he created Walcher, the first Norman bishop of Durham, Earl of Northumberland and gave him civil authority over this part of England. In return, Walcher promised to defend the border separating the English from the Scots. Thus commenced the joint civil-spiritual jurisdiction which made the holder of the Durham bishopric an absolute prince with powers and privileges similar to the king's.

In the 12th century, Bishop Hugh Pudsey rebuilt William's castle, and every century following saw further additions and alterations: Bishop Bek in the 13th century, Bishop Hatfield in the 14th, Bishop Fox in the 15th, Bishop Tunstall in the 16th, and, finally, Bishop Cosin in the 17th century, all left their marks on Durham Castle. Until 1836, the castle was the home of Durham's prince-bishops.

Enter the grounds of the castle through the great **Gatehouse,** with its massive 16th-century oak-and-iron doors. Parts of the Gatehouse are original 12th-century work, although the upper portion was designed by the late-18th-century architect James Wyatt. From the Gatehouse, enter the **Castle Courtyard,** which is surrounded by a picturesque assortment of buildings representing the nine centuries of the castle's existence. To your extreme right is the round keep rebuilt in 1840 on the site of the original 14th-century keep (it now houses college students). Next to the keep on the left is Tunstall's 16th-century Chapel, with Pudsey's 12th-century building occupying the remainder of this north side of the castle. In the angle between the north and west façades is Bishop Cosin's 17th-century stairway, and the entire west side of the castle contains the 13th-century Great Hall and the Tudor kitchens.

Walk to your left toward the magnificent Ionic doorway built by Bishop Cosin in the mid-17th century. Guided tours through the castle are given frequently and begin just beyond this entrance (hours: July to September and the first three weeks in April, 10–12, 2–4:30; rest of the year, Monday, Wednesday, and Saturday, 2–4:30). You will see first the tremendous late-15th–early-16th-century **kitchen** with its huge fireplaces; the kitchen has been used for almost five hundred years, and even today meals for University College students are still prepared here. You then enter the **Great Hall,** built in 1284 by Bishop Antony Bek. The spectacular open timber roof was added sixty-six years later by Bishop Thomas Hatfield, and the minstrels' gallery in 1500 by Bishop Richard Fox. This magnificent dining hall, reputed to be the finest college dining hall in England, has entertained many famous guests, including Sir Walter Scott and the Duke of Wellington, who both dined here in 1827 as guests of Bishop William van Mildert. Nowadays, it is still used as a dining hall by the students of University College.

From the north end of the Great Hall, you climb Bishop Cosin's **Black Staircase** of beautifully carved oak to **Bishop Tunstall's Gallery.** This Gallery was constructed between 1530 and 1559 in front of Bishop Pudsey's 12th-century building to provide access to Bishop Tunstall's chapel, and is a splendid example of Tudor architecture. Two-thirds of the way down the Gallery on the left is the magnificent late Norman doorway which was once the main entrance to Bishop Pudsey's castle. From this Gallery you reach the **Tunstall Chapel,** another good example of the Tudor style. This chapel replaced the Norman chapel and was subsequently enlarged in 1700 by Bishop Lord Crewe. The oak stalls from the early 16th century are remarkable, and some display interesting carvings—particularly those beneath the seats in the northwest corner. Note the carving under the first seat, of a man pushing a wheelbarrow with a woman seated in it.

Now return to the Black Staircase and walk up to the **Norman Gallery,** a relic of Bishop Pudsey's building. Be sure to examine the interesting arcades along the south and west walls. The view from the windows is exciting. Next you visit the tiny **Norman Chapel,** probably the earliest existing portion of the castle. The herringbone-patterned pavement, the groined vaulting, as well as the capitals decorated with animals, plants, and geometric designs, are all late-11th-century.

For 750 years this castle was the home of the prince-bishops of Durham. In 1832, an Act of Parliament created Durham University, the third university in England (after Oxford and Cambridge). The last prince-bishop, William van Mildert, gave his castle and much of his revenue to the fledgling university.

University College, which now occupies the castle and most of the buildings surrounding Palace Green, became the first of the present 14 colleges associated with Durham University.

From the castle, return to Owen-Gate and then turn right to walk along **North Bailey,** once part of the town's fortifications, and now lined with lovely 18th-century Georgian townhouses. On the right side of the street at the junction of North Bailey and Owen-Gate is a mid-19th-century building which was once the site of the Halmote Court, which handled minor misdemeanors and petty debts since the mid-14th century. This court ceased functioning only in 1952.

On the opposite side of the street is **Hatfield College,** the second-oldest college of Durham University, founded in 1846. Opposite the entrance gates you can see what was once a coaching inn called the Red Lion; the fireplace from this inn was moved to the Mayor's Chamber in the Town Hall. To the left of the gateway is the Victorian chapel, and a few steps farther along North Bailey is the church of **St. Mary-le-Bow.** This church takes its name from the "bow" or arch which once spanned Bow Lane just around the corner, and which, with the church's bell tower, formed an inner defense for the castle and cathedral. In 1637 the bell tower collapsed, destroying both the arch and much of the church nave. St. Mary-le-Bow was rebuilt in 1685.

Turn left on Bow Lane and walk toward the river. Directly in front of you is the elegant modern **footbridge** erected in 1963 by Ove Arup to connect the suburb of Elvet to the peninsula. Walk midway across this daring bridge; on the opposite side you see Dunelm House, built in 1965 as a student union and social center. Now turn around and return to the peninsula: To your right is the 17th-century house occupied by the Master of Hatfield College, and to your left is a portion of the old city wall which once enclosed the peninsula.

Continue along Bow Lane to North Bailey and cross the street to **Dun Cow Lane,** a quaint little lane which leads back to Palace Green. Dun Cow Lane takes its name from the ancient legend revolving around the 10th-century Bishop Aldhun. The bishop was seeking a site for the church, which was to serve as a shrine to northern England's most famous saint, Cuthbert. He was led to the promontory high above the River Wear by a dun (neutral-colored) cow. The bishop took this as a sign that his church should be built on this promontory—and so it was. This Saxon cathedral became the resting place and shrine for St. Cuthbert's remains. Cuthbert's story is fascinating, particularly the tale of the meandering of his body after his death. Cuthbert was a 7th-century monk who became prior and later bishop of the Benedictine monastery on the island of Landisfarne off the coast of Northumberland. He spent his last years living in isolation as a hermit and, before he died in 687, made his Benedictine followers promise to take his body with them should they ever be forced to leave their island monastery. The time came in 875, 188 years after Cuthbert's death, when Viking raids on the island forced the monks to migrate south. They were faithful to their promise made two centuries earlier and took Cuthbert's body with them. After wandering for eight years, the monks settled in Chester-le-Street, where they remained for 112 years. In 995, fresh Viking raids forced another migration, and they headed south again, where, it is said, the cow led them to the Durham peninsula and where Cuthbert's coffin, still being carted about, rooted itself to the ground.

Bishop Aldhun, Durham's first bishop, built his cathedral shrine for Cuthbert's body. The Danish King Canute, who also became England's king in 1016, supposedly visited this shrine in 1031 to pay homage to the saint. A hundred years after Aldhun had completed his church, Bishop William of St. Calais began construction in 1093 on what was to become one of the finest Norman buildings in Europe. His work was completed a bare 40 years later by Bishop Ranulf Flambard, although there were subsequent additions, such as the Galilee Porch and the Chapel of the Nine Altars. The two western towers were built between 1150 and 1225, and the present central tower, which can be climbed, is 218 feet high and belongs to the late 15th century. It replaced an earlier tower destroyed by lightning.

As you approach the church along its north side, look for the carved figure of a cow on the northwest corner of the east end of the cathedral, the end called the Chapel of the Nine Altars. This is Bishop Aldhun's famous dun cow. Walk to the Norman north door, the main entrance to the church, with its huge beast's head. This 12th-century bronze head is a **sanctuary knocker:** Anyone who grasped it was given refuge—even murderers. Fugitives were allowed to remain in the cathedral for 37 days; if they hadn't cleared up their affairs by then, they were given safe passage to the coast and were then on their own. The cathedral's records show that, in the 60 years between 1464 and 1524, 331 people availed themselves of sanctuary.

Entering the cathedral through this north door, you are in the north aisle, where you can clearly see one of the many features for which this church is renowned. Durham Cathedral was one of the first churches in Europe to use stone-ribbed vaulting, and this north aisle and its twin to the south were both constructed in the early part of the 12th century. Walk to the center aisle for a marvelous perspective on the nave, one of the few examples of pure Romanesque style in England (Peterborough and Norwich are two others). The 18th-century writer Dr. Samuel Johnson called this view one of "rocky solidity and indeterminate duration." It is simple and yet grand, a superb example of uncluttered majesty. Notice the two types of pillars alternating down the body of the church: circular columns rich with geometric designs alternating with clustered piers around a central pillar.

Directly behind you on the floor is the black marble cross called the **boundary cross,** beyond which no woman could venture; women were restricted to the extreme west end of the cathedral. Durham Cathedral was attached to a Benedictine monastery and the monks might have found the presence of women disturbing. There is also a rumor that Cuthbert, despite his abundant saintly qualities, was a professed woman-hater. A story is told about the time when Bishop Hugh Pudsey began building the Lady Chapel, in 1175, at the usual east end of the church, adjacent to Cuthbert's shrine. Strange cracks developed in the walls, and this was interpreted as a sign that Cuthbert disapproved even of a chapel to the Blessed Virgin so close to him. The Lady Chapel was built at the unorthodox west end. It's a good thing you didn't have to be passed by a feminist board to be elected saint in those days!

Behind the boundary cross is the alabaster **baptismal font** with its elaborate wood canopy, given by the 17th-century bishop, John Cosin. The lovely west window dates from 1346. Enter the

Lady Chapel, popularly called the **Galilee Porch.** This example of late Norman architecture has a slightly Moorish flavor because of the elegant frilled stonework on the arches. The most famous occupant of the Galilee Porch is the Venerable Bede, the 8th-century scholar and cleric who wrote the *Ecclesiastical History of the English People,* the earliest surviving English history. Bede died at the monastery at Jarrow in 735. Three centuries later, Aelfred, a monk associated with Durham Cathedral, stole Bede's bones and brought them to Durham. Bede's resting place is marked by a simple slab with the inscription: HÂC SUNT IN FOSSÂ BAEDAE VENERABILIS OSSA ("Here in this hole are the bones of the Venerable Bede"). To Bede's left is the tomb of the 15th-century bishop Thomas Langley, who was both cardinal and twice Chancellor of England. The painting of the Crucifixion above Bishop Langley's tomb dates back to the 13th century.

Return to the nave and walk along the south aisle to see what was once the **Neville Chantry,** containing the battered tombs of several Lord Nevilles. Ralph Lord Neville who was the commander of the army which, in 1345, defeated the Scots at Neville's Cross, just one mile outside the city, was the first layman to be buried in the cathedral. His son, John, and a descendent, Bishop Robert Neville, rest close by. In 1650, Oliver Cromwell incarcerated 4,000 Scottish prisoners in the cathedral after the Battle of Dunbar. It was these men who mutilated the Neville Chantry and also burned the choir stalls to keep themselves warm.

Now proceed to the south transept to see the 15th-century stained glass window and the beautiful late-15th-century clock case; the dials and the clockworks were renewed in 1632. In the southwest corner is the entrance to the central tower. If you want to climb up 218 feet, the view over Durham and the countryside is well worth it. In the transept crossing is the ornate **pulpit** resting on small lions designed by Sir George Gilbert Scott. Sir George, one of the most notable Victorian architects of the Gothic revival in England, also designed the huge Albert Memorial in London.

To your right adjacent to the pulpit is Sir George's alabaster-and-marble screen which divides the nave from the choir. Pass into the choir between the splendid 17th-century **choir stalls** installed by Bishop Cosin. On your right is one of the cathedral's highlights, the spectacular **Bishop's Throne.** The lower portion of the throne serves as a tiny chantry for the tomb of Bishop Thomas Hatfield, the originator of the throne, who died in 1381. The upper portion is literally the "highest throne in Christendom." The gilt and color on the lower portion add to its magnificence. Behind the high altar is the light, airy stone **altar screen** which was the gift of John Lord Neville in the late 14th century. The screen was once adorned with 107 gilded and painted statues, but these were destroyed in the Dissolution of the churches and monasteries under Henry VIII. Those statues which escaped destruction were then smashed to pieces by Cromwell's army.

Go behind the high altar into the **Chapel of the Nine Altars,** so named because it once contained nine altars set up against the east wall. This chapel, with its pointed arches and carved capitals, is an excellent example of the Early English Gothic style and was built in the middle of the 13th century to replace an earlier Norman apse. Behind the altar screen once stood the elaborate shrine of St. Cuthbert, which was visited during the Middle Ages by numerous kings, queens, and noblemen (including Henry VI and Richard III), all bearing handsome gifts. It was destroyed in 1540, during the Dissolution, and now the saint's body rests beneath a plain marble slab simply inscribed with his name, Cuthbertus. The great east window is neo-Gothic, the work of the 18th-century architect James Wyatt. Wyatt had great plans for altering the cathedral, including pulling down the Galilee Porch. Fortunately, public indignation prevented him from accomplishing this. He did, however, manage to damage much of the cathedral by paring away at the stone exterior. At the north end is a statue of Bishop William van Mildert, the last of Durham's prince-bishops and the founder of Durham University.

Return to the transept crossing, stopping for a moment in the north transept to see the 14th-century north window and the roof vaulting, which is 850 years old. Now walk down the nave, pass the Neville Chantry, and look for the door called the Monks' Door, off the south aisle. Note the remarkable 12th-century ironwork on this doorway, which leads to the **cloisters.**

These cloisters were added long after the cathedral was completed, at the end of the 14th and the beginning of the 15th centuries. Walk along the north and east sides of the cloisters to visit the 12th-century **Chapter House,** one of the finest Norman structures in the country. This building was partially destroyed in 1796 during Wyatt's "restoration," and was rebuilt to its original shape in 1895. From the Chapter House, walk all the way around to reach the **Monks' Dormitory.** This great timbered hall, built at the same time as the cloisters, is now a fascinating museum. The late-7th-century wooden coffin in which St. Cuthbert was carried about until he finally came to his resting place in Durham is displayed here, as well as some 10th-century Anglo-Saxon vestments, supposedly the gift of King Athelstan, which are the oldest examples of needlework in England. You can also see a unique collection of Saxon crosses and medieval illuminated manuscripts.

Leave the cathedral by the north door and turn right to walk once more down Dun Cow Lane to North Bailey. Turn right, and across the street is **St. Chad's College,** which occupies a Georgian building. St. Chad's is a theological college associated with Durham University. North Bailey becomes **South Bailey,** another lovely street lined with more 18th-century Georgian structures. At one time, many of these Georgian buildings were private residences of wealthy Durham citizens. A bit farther on is **St. John's College,** another theological school occupying a number of Georgian buildings. Across the street from St. John's is the 16th-century Gatehouse, leading to the large open courtyard called "the College," once the monastery's courtyard but now surrounded by the lovely homes of church dignitaries. Past the Gatehouse, on the right, is the church of **St. Mary-the-Less,** originally built by the wealthy Neville family in the 12th century. The church was completely restored in 1846, and now serves as the chapel of St. John's College. Step inside for a moment to see the Norman carving of Christ Glorified over the doorway on the north side of the choir.

Stroll slowly downhill along South Bailey and pass beneath the 18th-century Water Gate. In front of you is **Prebend's Bridge,** one of the loveliest bridges crossing the Wear. There was a ferry here during the Middle Ages. Later a footbridge was built, which was carried away in the great flood of 1771. The present bridge was constructed between 1772 and 1778, and inscribed on it are Sir Walter Scott's famous lines describing Durham Cathedral:

> Grey towers of Durham
> Yet well I love thy mixed and massive piles
> Half church of God, half castle 'gainst the Scot
> And long to roam these venerable aisles
> With records stored of deeds long since forgot.

From the bridge you have a breathtaking view of Durham Cathedral's towers. To the north is Framwelgate Bridge, where you began your walking tour, and off to the right, beneath the mass of the cathedral, you can see the picturesque old **corn mill** beside the weir, which now houses the University's Department of Archaeology.

From Prebend's Bridge, take the first left turn toward the cathedral, following the path called Broken Walls. To the right you see a portion of the old City Wall which once encircled the peninsula. This wall was used as a quarry for houses and shops, hence its name: Broken Walls. Follow the path beneath the west end of the cathedral and the castle until you emerge close to Framwelgate Bridge. Cross the bridge and continue on the first street to your left, South Street, which climbs a steep hill. From the top of this hill, you have a magnificent final view of the castle and cathedral with its twin west towers and the Galilee Porch. You can then descend via a pathway toward the river and Prebend's Bridge. The perfect way to end your walking tour of Durham is to stroll leisurely along the bank of the Wear, enjoying the wonders of nature and man's achievement which combine to make Durham unique and unforgettable.

* * *

Before leaving Durham, plan a short excursion to a special museum, the **Gulbenkian Museum of Oriental Art and Archaeology** (hours: Monday to Friday, 9:30–1, 2:15–5; Saturday, 9:30–12, 2:15–5; Sunday, 2:15–5; from Christmas to Easter, the museum is closed Saturday, and Sunday afternoon). It's only about a mile's walk from Kingsgate Bridge, but you can also drive or take a cab. If you walk, follow Church Street, which begins at Kingsgate Bridge. Church Street runs into South Road. Walk along South Road until you come to Elvet Hill Road on the right. A short distance ahead, on the left, you'll see the entrance to the museum. The Gulbenkian Museum is the only museum in England devoted exclusively to Oriental art. You'll see Egyptian tomb furnishings, Chinese jades and porcelain, Tibetan paintings, and Indian bronze sculpture. It seems a little peculiar to wander among this treasurehouse of Eastern art after exploring a superb medieval, Tudor, and Georgian city, but the collection is outstanding and shouldn't be missed.

EXETER

Exeter has the distinction of being the one English city which has been continuously inhabited from pre-Roman times to the present day. While other Roman cities were eclipsed in the so-called Dark Ages under Anglo-Saxon and Danish kings, Exeter thrived. The Romans built the City Walls, the Normans built the castle, the great church builders of the 13th and 14th centuries built the splendid Gothic cathedral, the common people built the lovely Tudor houses and quaint Elizabethan inns, and the patricians of the 17th and 18th centuries built mansions off the city's main thoroughfares. Despite wars, insurrections, and other conflicts, much of this building remains today for you to enjoy.

Exeter's history is similar to that of many other English towns. Before the Romans, Celtic peoples had settled here beside the river. The Romans named the settlement Isca Dumnoniorum, built the walls, and settled in for several hundred years. After the Romans, there were several centuries of quiet until the invading Danes besieged the town in 876. King Alfred drove them out a few years later, but the Danes tried again in 1003, and this time they destroyed the cathedral. Exeter fell to William the Conqueror in 1068. During the 12th and 13th centuries, the city thrived on its dual status as leading cloth-manufacturing center and important seaport, a status which it lost for several hundred years and then regained in the 16th century. Exeter was involved in every war of the 15th, 16th, and 17th centuries. Charles I lived here for a time while fighting Cromwell's armies; his daughter, Henrietta, was born here. Charles II came to Exeter after the Restoration to thank the city for its royalist loyalties during the Civil War. Exeter has never remained in the background of English history. Unfortunately, this meant that every war took its toll on the city, even in this century, when it received more than its share of Nazi bombs. But Exeter survived, recuperated, and thrived, as it has for more than two thousand years.

Stroll through this ancient English city, which has been home equally to Celt, Roman, Saxon, Norman, and the present-day Englishman who is an amalgam of this varied and rich past. Enjoy the contrast of 3rd-century Roman walls next to 18th-century Georgian houses, half-timbered Tudor shops shouldering modern storefronts, 17th-century public gardens on the site of an 11th-century castle—they are all part of the rich fabric which is Exeter.

Begin your walk through Exeter in front of its magnificent **Cathedral,** considered a superlative example of the English Middle Gothic or Decorated Gothic style. King Athelstan built a monastic church on this site in 932. In their second invasion of Devon in 1003, the Danes destroyed Athelstan's church, but Canute, the Danish leader, who became king of England in 1016, rebuilt the church shortly after he was crowned. In 1050, Edward the Confessor made Exeter a bishopric and appointed Leofric as first bishop; both Edward and his queen, Edytha, came to Exeter to witness Leofric's installation. In 1068, William the Conqueror conquered Exeter, and forty years later Bishop William Warelwast replaced Canute's monastic edifice with a massive Norman structure. All that remains of Bishop Warelwast's church are the two sturdy transeptal towers, unique in English cathedral architecture. Late in the 13th century, the Norman church began to be transformed into the lovely Gothic building you see before you today. The transformation, begun by Bishop Walter Bronescombe, was continued by his four successors to its completion by Bishop John Grandisson about the year 1369.

Step back far enough to see the entire **west front** with the two Norman towers on either side of the nave. The tower on the north side, called the St. Paul Tower, contains a six-ton bell, "Great Peter," one of the largest in the world. It has been tolling the curfew at the end of each day for the past 500 years. The great west window is relatively new, since World War II, and contains figures of individuals prominent in the history of the cathedral, including its Gothic builders. But the highlight of this façade is the panoply of **sculptured figures**—apostles, angels, saints, prophets, and kings—which fill the lower half of this west front.

Enter the cathedral through its main doorway. In front of you

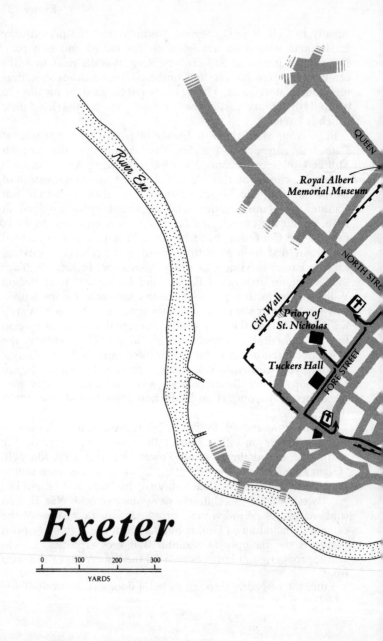

River Exe

QUEEN

Royal Albert
Memorial Museum

NORTH STRE

City Wall

Priory of
St. Nicholas

Tuckers Hall

FORE STREET

Exeter

0   100   200   300

YARDS

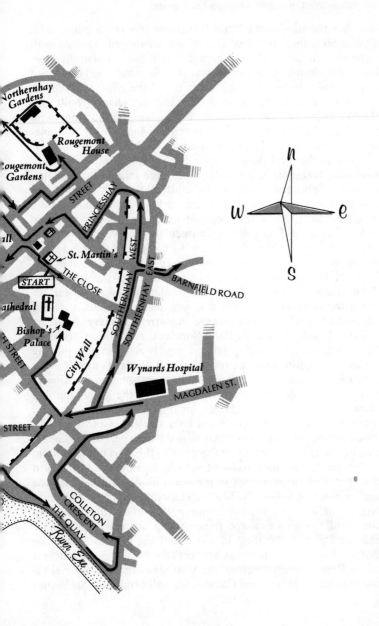

stretches the nave, with Purbeck marble pillars on either side. Over it all is three hundred feet of remarkable rib-vaulted **roof,** unbroken in perspective except for the great organ halfway down the church. You can almost imagine that you've stepped into an aisle shaded by stone palm trees—the effect is splendid. Just to the right of the main door is the tiny **chantry** built into the thickness of the west wall by Bishop Grandisson, who witnessed the completion of the century-long labor of transforming the cathedral from Norman to Gothic.

Close to the west door to your right is the late-17th-century **baptismal font,** with a cover displaying the inlaid figures of the Apostles. Behind the font on the south wall is the colorful flag carried by Captain Robert Scott on his expedition to the Antarctic in 1900; Capt. Scott died on a second Antarctic expedition in 1912. If you have binoculars with you and if there is enough light in the church, try to locate the exquisite **boss** (keystone at the intersection of the rib vaulting) in the roof between the first and second pillars, depicting the murder of Archbishop Thomas à Becket of Canterbury. A little farther down the nave on the north side you come to another of this cathedral's unique features, the **minstrel's gallery** built by Bishop Grandisson for the Palm Sunday ceremonies. Carved on the front of this lovely gallery are twelve angels playing medieval English instruments: from left to right, the citole (a type of lute), bagpipes, recorder, rebec (viol), harp, Jew's harp, trumpet, hand organ, gittern (a member of the guitar family), shawm (double-reed woodwind instrument), tambourine, and cymbals. Today the gallery is used for Christmas-carol recitals. Needlepoint devotees will have noticed the spectacular collection of colorful kneelers in all the pews in this part of the church.

Proceed to the **south transept,** which, together with the north transept, was reconstructed in the late 13th century beneath the earlier Norman towers. Notice the elaborate tracery in the south window and the exquisite triforium gallery above the arcade. In the middle of this transept rests Hugh Courtenay, the second Earl of Devon, who died in 1377, and his wife, Margaret de Bohun. Two swans mourn at her feet (the swan was the emblem of the Bohun family). Behind the Courtenay tomb to the right is the monument of Sir John Gilbert, the half brother of Sir Walter

Raleigh, who died in 1596. This is a bad corner to be caught in during an organ recital, which you will immediately realize if you glance to your right. Also in this corner is the entrance to the **Chapter House,** once used by the Dean of the cathedral for administrative meetings. The beautiful ceiling here dates from the late 15th century. You will be surprised, perhaps unpleasantly, to see modern sculpture emerging from the medieval arcades along both walls.

Return to the nave. In front of you is the triple-arched **stone screen** erected by Bishop Walter de Stapeldon early in the 14th century to separate the nave from the choir area. The paintings along the top of the screen are from the 17th century, and so is the huge organ, which was installed in this controversial position above the screen in 1665. Although the organ blocks our view of the great east window, it serves as a useful break to the 300-foot length of the roof.

Go beneath the screen into the choir. Although the choir stalls are the product of 19th-century craftsmanship, the **misericords** (the hinged seats with the bracket beneath) are six centuries older, and are believed to be the oldest in England. They are also rather amusing: There's a king sitting in boiling water, a boat being towed by a swan, and an elephant with cowlike hooves. Here also is the elaborate **Bishop's Throne,** carved in 1316 for Bishop Stapeldon by Thomas of Winchester.

As you walk toward the main altar, notice the noble **east window** with its original 14th-century stained glass. To the left of the main altar is the tomb of Bishop Stapeldon, the 14th-century prelate who was responsible for so much of this beautiful choir area. Bishop Stapeldon was lord high treasurer to the unpopular King Edward III. His loyalty to this king cost him his life at the hands of a London mob in 1326. To the right of the altar is a group of seats reserved for clergy, called the **sedilia.** These date from the early 14th century and have lacy, filigreelike canopies. The statues are modern and represent Edward the Confessor, Exeter's first bishop, Leofric, and Edward's queen, Edytha.

Leave the choir and walk along the south aisle toward the east end of the cathedral. On the right side you pass the early-16th-century chantry of Bishop Oldham, which is profusely decorated with owls. The owl might have been his favorite bird, or perhaps the good bishop considered himself as "wise as an owl." It is more likely, however, that the bishop's name was pronounced "Owldham."

At the east end of the cathedral is the Lady Chapel, one of the first sections of the church to be rebuilt in the late 13th century. By the entrance to the chapel is a late-15th-century fresco of the Assumption. Just inside the chapel on the south side is the splendid, delicately carved, 15th-century **tomb of Bishop Walter Bronescombe.** The bishop, who initiated the transformation of the cathedral from Norman to Gothic, died in 1280, 200 years before his tomb was carved. Notice his painted effigy. Peter de Quivel, his successor, continued the transformation; he rests in front of the altar. Just to the right is the tomb of another early bishop, possibly Exeter's first bishop, Leofric. On the north side of the Lady Chapel are the imposing tombs of Sir John Dodderidge and his wife, who both died in the early 17th century.

Walk along the north choir aisle to the north transept, which is as beautiful in its window tracery and triforium gallery as its twin across the way. In the northeast corner is the minuscule 16th-century Sylke Chantry. Above the chantry is an interesting late-15th-century **fresco** of the Resurrection, depicting a church sexton rushing off with his spade, his wife following with a lantern. Notice also the expressions on the soldiers' faces. On the opposite side of the transept is the 15th-century **clock** with two dials, one with minutes, and the more curious one with a geocentric universe showing the moon revolving around the earth, and the sun revolving around both of them.

Return up the nave toward the west door. Before leaving the cathedral, see the tablet and stained glass window to the right of the west door in memory of Richard Blackmore, the 19th-century author of *Lorna Doone,* which is set in the nearby Devon moorland.

Leave the cathedral and take the path across the grass to the right where you see the statue of the 16th-century theologian Richard Hooker, a native of Heavitree, now a suburb of Exeter. The church in front of you is **St. Martin's,** dedicated in 1065 by Leofric. The interior of this church is largely 15th- and 17th-century work: The west window is 15th century, and the woodwork is 17th. Leave St. Martin's, turn left, and you are in the area called **The Close,** full of attractive old stone and wooden-timbered houses. Next door to the church is **Mol's Coffee House,** which actually served in that capacity between 1596 and 1663, and is now an art shop. Many famous seafaring men of the early 17th century, including Sir Walter Raleigh, Sir Francis Drake, and Sir John Hawkins, liked to come to Mol's after their voyages to spin a yarn (the port of Plymouth is only thirty-five miles away). You can go up to the first floor to see the room in which these adventurers used to sit and sip.

The house at No. 9 has an interesting 14th-century hall with a lovely carved roof which you can see from the passageway between Nos. 7 and 9. At No. 10 is a stone archway with a massive, carved oak door which leads to a small quadrangle and the Bishop of Crediton's residence. In 1501, Catherine of Aragon, on her way to marry Prince Arthur, heir to the English throne, and Henry VIII's brother, stayed in the house next door on her first night in England, and, 187 years later, William of Orange lived in this same house for twelve days before proceeding to London.

Return along The Close past Mol's and St. Martin's. Directly ahead is the narrow Martins Lane, and to the right is the famous 14th-century pub **Ship Inn.** When Raleigh, Drake, and Hawkins weren't sipping coffee at Mol's, they were here downing their pints of ale; with all this drinking of various sorts these three did, it's a wonder they ever got around to adventuring! Raleigh loved this inn so well that he wrote, in a letter dated 1587: "Next to mine own Shippe I do most love that Old Shippe in Exon [Exeter], a tavern in St. Martins Lane." You might want to stop off now or return later on to follow their good example and down your own pint.

Continue along Martins Lane to **High Street,** Exeter's main street which follows the 2,000-year-old Roman road down to the River Exe. This street, along with much of Exeter, was badly bombed during World War II; thank goodness much was also spared. Across the street to the left you see one of Exeter's most famous buildings, the **Guildhall.** The present structure, said to be the oldest municipal building in use in England, was built in 1330, although a Town Hall existed here as early as the 12th century. The sturdy stone portico projecting out over the sidewalk was added in 1593. Go inside (hours: Monday to Saturday, 9–5:30, except when the building is being used for meetings) to see the fine wooden roof added in 1470. The carved brackets bear the arms of Warwick, "the Kingmaker." Richard Neville, Earl of Warwick, was a 15th-century politician related to both the Yorkists and the Lancastrians, who fought the War of the Roses for possession of the English crown. Neville supported one side first and then the other, and it was said that he was more powerful than the king at this time—hence his nickname, "the Kingmaker." The walls of the hall were paneled in oak in 1594 and are adorned with the arms of various guilds and mayors. There is a portrait of Charles II's sister, Princess Henrietta, born in Exeter in 1644 while her father, Charles I, was fighting Parliamentary armies in the Great Civil War. Ask to see the two regal swords, one belonging to Edward IV, the other to Henry VII. They are the only swords actually used by English kings which are still in existence.

Next door to the Guildhall is the medieval pub called **The Turks Head,** which has paid for the privilege of being shoulder to shoulder with the Guildhall since 1289—Guild members make thirsty customers! This inn is rich in Dickensian associations: It is said that Dickens discovered his famous Fat Boy Joe *(Pickwick Papers)* while dining here.

A little farther along High Street on the right is **Parliament Street,** claiming to be the narrowest street in England. It's only two to four feet wide. Parliament Street used to lead to the most ancient church in Exeter, **St. Pancras,** which has an 11th-century Norman baptismal font and pulpit. As of this writing, the area behind Parliament Street is under construction. The reader will have to figure out how to reach the church if he wishes to visit it. Return to High Street and turn right. Across the street is another old church, St. Petrock, with a Norman tower.

After a few more steps, High Street becomes Fore Street. Make a right turn on Mary Arches Street, and on your right is the 12th-century parish church of **St. Mary Arches,** the least changed Norman church in all of Devon. Go inside to see its unique double arcade and the tomb of Thomas Walker, three times mayor of Exeter. Return to Fore Street and turn right. On the right you pass another ancient church, St. Olave's. The patroness of this church was Gytha, the mother of Harold II, who was defeated by William the Conqueror at the Battle of Hastings in 1066.

A little farther along on the right, you come to the street called The Mint, where you will find the **Priory of St. Nicholas.** This Benedictine priory, established in the year 1070 by William the Conqueror, was once the most important monastic foundation in Exeter. It was dissolved in 1535, during the reign of Henry VIII. You can tour what's left of the monastic buildings (hours: April to September, Monday to Saturday, 10–1, 2–5:30; October to March, priory closes at 4) to see the 11th-century Undercroft, the kitchen, the Prior's Cell, and the Guest Hall, a 15th-century communal dormitory. In the tiny garden of the priory is a Celtic cross shaft more than 1,100 years old.

Once more continue down Fore Street. At No. 140 you come to another guildhall, **Tuckers Hall,** which belonged to the shearmen, weavers, and fullers (whose job was to shrink and then thicken wool cloth). This guildhall was built in 1471, and you can go inside (hours: June to September, Tuesday, Thursday, and Friday, 10:30–12:30; rest of the year, Friday only, 10:30–12:30) to see the splendid late-15th-century roof. The fireplace and the oak paneling date from the early 17th century.

Walk to the bottom of Fore Street and turn left into steep **West Street,** one of the oldest streets in the city. Halfway down on your left is the parish church of **St. Mary Steps,** with its quaint 17th-century bell-tower clock with figures that strike the hours. Across from the church was once the Westgate, the medieval city gate. This has since disappeared, but you should make a short detour up the picturesque, steep, cobblestoned **Stepcote Hill,** which was once the main thoroughfare from the Westgate to High Street. This street hasn't changed much in the last seven hundred years.

Return to West Street and take a look at some of the fine 16th-century houses next to the church. Across the street, at No. 24, is the half-timbered house known as the **House That Moved,** because it was recently moved seventy-five yards from Frog Street to this site due to road construction. The structure dates from the 14th century, and is supposed to be one of the oldest timber-framed buildings in England.

Continue along West Street to Lower Coombe Street on your

right. As you stroll down this street you see to your left a section of the old **City Walls** built by the Romans about the year 200. King Athelstan strengthened these walls in the early 10th century, and in some places they are ten feet wide. At the end of the street on your right you'll see the **Custom House.** This 1682 building is a very early example of the use of brickwork in Exeter. Exeter was once a thriving port, and goods on the way up the River Exe were unloaded here for inspection. Continue a short distance ahead to visit the **Quay,** with its picturesque, tall warehouses, further evidence of Exeter's past importance as a center of commerce. Continue strolling along the Quay, passing the Exeter Maritime Museum (hours: summer, 10–6; winter, 10–5), until you come to Colleton Hill, the first street on your left. Walk up the hill and take the first left turn, into **Colleton Crescent,** a marvelous survivor of Georgian England. The street is lined with attractive Georgian houses of the late 18th century.

At the end of Colleton Crescent, follow Friars Gate to the right until you come to the busy Magdalen Street. Across the street to the right is **Wynards Hospital,** founded in 1430 by William Wynard, the chief judicial magistrate of Exeter, to support a dozen infirm poor. Take a look at the lovely cobblestoned courtyard surrounded by medieval buildings. These structures served as almshouses for more than 500 years (until 1970) and, appropriately enough, now house the city's social services.

From Wynards, turn right and walk toward the intersection of four of the city's busiest streets, and take the street to the right, South Street. On your left you pass the **White Hart Inn,** an ancient establishment which has been serving food and grog since the 14th century. On the right enter Palace Gate, and you are back in the precincts of the cathedral. Toward the east end of the cathedral is the 14th-century Bishop's Palace, housing the **Cathedral Library** (hours: Monday to Friday, 2–5). Here you can examine the 11th-century Exeter Domesday manuscript, the survey of the southwestern counties undertaken by William the Conqueror in 1086, and the 10th-century collection of Anglo-Saxon poetry known as the Exeter Codex.

Return to the intersection, turn left, and then make another left along Southernhay East. Again bear left, onto **Southernhay West,** one of Exeter's loveliest streets, lined with 18th-century

Georgian houses and flowerbeds. Continue strolling along Southernhay West until you come to Barnfield Road on your right. Follow Barnfield Road to **Barnfield Crescent** on the left, another charming Georgian street with late-18th-century houses.

Return to Southernhay West, turn right, and at the end turn left. Straight ahead you will see the entrance to one of the city's most unusual sights, the **Underground Passages** (hours: Monday to Friday, 2–5). Dating from the 14th century, these passages once housed the conduits carrying the city's water supply from the nearby Longbrook Valley. They were still being used until one hundred years ago. After leaving the Passages, walk a few feet and turn left along **Princesshay,** one of Exeter's most modern shopping centers, reserved for pedestrians only.

At the end of Princesshay, turn right along Bedford Street, which leads to High Street. Make a left. At the Church of St. Stephen go under the arch nicknamed "Stephen's Bow" to a secluded little courtyard, where you might want to rest a few minutes before continuing. Surrounding you are the remains of a 15th-century almshouse bombed out during World War II. Return to High Street, turn left, and continue on to Queen Street. Turn right and walk to the **Royal Albert Memorial Museum** (hours: Monday to Saturday, 10–5:30). Founded in 1865, this museum is crowded with archeological and natural history, as well as costume exhibits. The art collection is housed on the first floor.

Leave the museum, turn left at the corner along Upper Paul Street and then right along Gandy Street. Turn left at the corner and follow Musgrave Row. On your left are steps leading to the public library. After walking up, turn right, then make a left on Castle Street to **Rougemont House,** a splendid Georgian townhouse just outside the gate tower of Rougemont Castle. The gate tower is all that is left of William the Conqueror's castle. On this knob of elevated land, the highest point in the city, the Saxons erected a fortification. Much later, William the Conqueror built a castle here, surrounded by a moat and defensive walls. At one time, this castle was considered a key position for defending Devon. So well known was Rougemont Castle in medieval and Elizabethan times that it is mentioned in Shakespeare's *Richard III,* when Richard himself says: "When last I was at Exeter, the mayor in courtesy show'd me the castle, and call'd it Rougemont." (Act IV, scene ii). Centuries passed, and the castle fell into ruins and was torn down, although you can still see traces of the moat, a medieval tower called Athelstan's Tower, and the Norman gate tower in front of you. If you go into Castle Yard, beyond the gate tower, you can see what was once the actual site of the castle. A late-18th-century Assize Court and county offices now occupy the site.

Return to Rougemont House, which now houses a museum (hours: Monday to Saturday, 10–1, 2–5:30) devoted to the archeology and history of Exeter from earliest times to the present day. From the museum, turn left and stroll into **Rougemont Gardens,** a pleasant park. Beyond the gardens stretches another lovely green area, **Northernhay Gardens,** bordered on one side by a fine section of the old City Walls. These are probably the oldest public gardens in England, having been laid out in the reign of Charles II, 300 years ago. It's a perfect spot to end your walk through the ancient city of Exeter—in Charles II's park, with the Roman walls and the ruins of a Norman castle nearby.

WARWICK

Warwick is set in the midst of some of England's greatest attractions: The honey-colored villages of the Cotswolds form a semicircle south of the city, Shakespeare's hometown of Stratford-upon-Avon is only a few miles away, and the modern cathedral of Coventry lies a short distance north. Perhaps for this reason, many tourists miss seeing Warwick. They run through Warwick Castle, one of England's most magnificent feudal castles, and well worth lingering in, but never really visit the town. Yet Warwick is a lovely small town with numerous Elizabethan stone and half-timbered houses, fine 17th- and 18th-century civic structures, and a beautiful collegiate church with a splendid Gothic chapel. And, of course, there is the castle, set above the River Avon, which towers over the town.

The history of Warwick is largely the history of its castle: The town's history is inextricably bound to the occupants of the castle. This history commences about the year 914, when Alfred the Great's daughter Ethelfleda built a fortress high above the Avon at a point where the river was spanned by a bridge. By the year 1086, twenty years after the Norman Conquest, Warwick is described in the Domesday Book, William the Conqueror's survey of his new English possessions, as a royal borough with over 200 houses. A few years later, another castle-fortress was built alongside Ethelfleda's fortress and the title of Earl of Warwick was created. Usually the earls occupied the castle, although there was a period in the 17th and 18th centuries when the Earls of Warwick did not own Warwick Castle. The involvement of Warwick in the fabric of English history is basically the involvement of these earls: the Beauchamps, the companions and sometimes the opponents of powerful kings, Richard Neville, at one time virtually King of England, Ambrose Dudley, brother of Queen Elizabeth's favorite, Robert Dudley, and the Grevilles.

Warwick is for strollers. It is small enough and picturesque enough that you will want to take your time and amble along

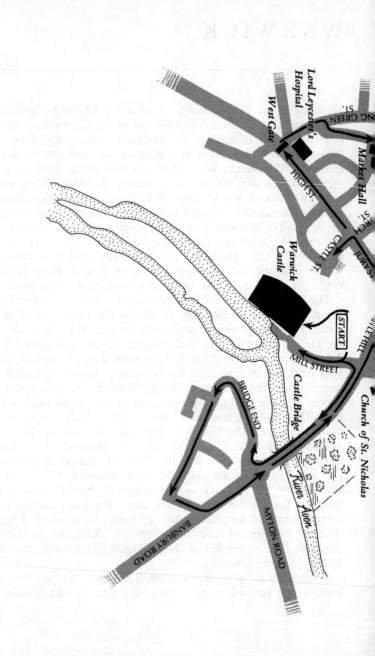

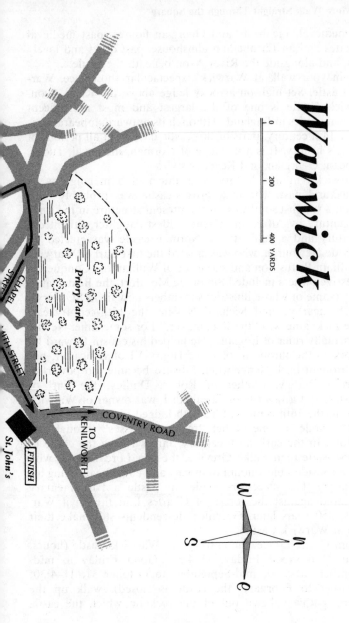

Warwick

0   200   400 YARDS

Priory Park

CHAPEL STREET

SMITH STREET

St. John's

FINISH

COVENTRY ROAD

TO KENILWORTH

W N
S E

past medieval, Jacobean, and Georgian houses, past medieval city gates and an Elizabethan almshouse, past quiet and lovely parks, and alongside the River Avon beneath the castle.

Begin your walk at Warwick's spectacular showpiece, **Warwick Castle.** Set high on a rocky ledge above the River Avon, Warwick Castle is one of the largest and most magnificent medieval castles in England. Although its outward appearance is largely 14th century, parts of this castle date from all periods of the city's history. It is a mélange of Norman, medieval, Tudor, Jacobean, Georgian, and Regency styles.

Warwick's human history is as much of a mélange as its architectural past. The first fortress-castle was probably built here on a site just southwest of the present structure in the early 10th century by Alfred the Great's oldest daughter, Ethelfleda. A century and a half later, a Norman castle was erected by Henry de Newburgh, who was created the first Earl of Warwick by William Rufus, son and successor of William the Conqueror. Successive owners included Simon de Montfort, the Beauchamp family (some of whose illustrious members now lie in St. Mary's Church, nearby), and Richard Neville, the 15th-century earl whose nickname was "the Kingmaker." For some time, Neville was virtually ruler of England. He helped his cousin Edward IV of York to the throne in place of Henry VI of Lancaster, but then brought back Henry when Edward became too powerful. Ambrose Dudley, brother of Robert Dudley, the Earl of Leicester, and a favorite of Elizabeth I, was owner of Warwick Castle in the 16th century. Elizabeth lodged in Warwick Castle in 1572 while on one of her "royal progresses" through her kingdom. In the early 17th century, James I gave the castle to the poet-statesman Fulke Greville, the first Lord Brooke, who spent a considerable amount of money and effort beautifying his new home. His successors made the castle a Parliamentary stronghold against the forces of Charles I in the Civil War. Today, 350 years later, Greville's descendents still make their home at Warwick Castle.

From Castle Lodge, the entrance to Warwick Castle (hours: March 1 to Good Friday, 11–4:30; Good Friday to mid-September, 10–5:30; mid-September to October 31, 11–4:30; November to February, the castle is closed), walk up the winding pathway hewn out of the rock on which the castle stands, to the double gateway. To your left is **Caesar's Tower,** 147 feet high, built in the mid-14th century by Thomas Beauchamp, who was also responsible for much of the castle's present-day appearance. To the right stands **Guy's Tower,** 128 feet high, but seemingly taller because it's set on a mound. It was built at the end of the 14th century by the second Thomas Beauchamp, son of the first Thomas.

Enter the castle's inner courtyard, with its thick, velvetlike lawn, and walk toward the left, where you will see the entrance to the **State Apartments,** which are packed with exquisite and priceless furniture, paintings, china, and armor. First you see the castle's **Chapel,** built by Fulke Greville early in the 17th century, with its two outstanding examples of Warwick woodcarving, the lectern and the altarpiece. Then proceed to the magnificent **Great Hall,** containing one of the finest collections of arms and armor in all of England including the suit of armor of Fulke Greville's successor who led the Parliamentary forces and was killed at the Battle of Lichfield in 1643. Notice the portrait of Elizabeth I in her coronation robes. In this room, Piers Gaveston, favorite of Edward II, was tried and condemned to death for treason in 1312. Because of his haughtiness, Gaveston had incurred the hatred of a powerful group of earls, including Guy Beauchamp, then Earl of Warwick. After his trial, the earls escorted Gaveston a mile and a half outside the city to Blacklow Hill and saw him beheaded. As you walk from room to room along this side of the castle, be sure to look out the windows for the spectacular view of the Avon below you. It was probably one of the last things the unfortunate Gaveston ever saw. The remains of a medieval bridge which once spanned the river are off to the left. Next on the itinerary is the **State Dining Room,** resplendent with white and gold paneling and a gilded ceiling. The painting dominating the room is a portrait of Charles I on horseback by Van Dyck. The picture of the lions above the fireplace is Rubens's work.

Next visit the very lovely **Red Drawing Room,** so called because of its red lacquered paneling. This room is richly decorated with masterpieces of art. There are two Van Dyck portraits, a Raphael portrait of Joanna, Queen of Naples, and a Rubens painting of the Marquis de Los Balbasses. Next is the elegant **Cedar Drawing Room,** with its 18th-century Adams fireplace, Aubusson carpet, and four Van Dyck portraits, including those of Charles I and his queen, Henrietta Maria. It seems rather strange that there should be so much of Charles I in this castle, considering that the second Lord Brooke supported Parliament against him. You come to the **Green Drawing Room,** with its unique Venetian table, inlaid with semiprecious stones, and Rubens's painting of the founder of the Jesuits, St. Ignatius Loyola, considered one of the finest paintings in the castle.

The **Queen Anne Bedroom** contains the bed slept in by this 18th-century monarch while she resided at Windsor Castle, and a portrait of the queen in her coronation robes. The tapestry dates from 1604 and was made in Brussels. Portraits of Anne's husband, George of Denmark, and son, the Duke of Gloucester, hang above the doors. The Duke of Gloucester was the only one of Anne's seventeen children to survive infancy, but he died at the age of twelve. Finally, you see the **Blue Boudoir,** with the very famous Holbein portrait of Henry VIII.

After your tour of the castle, be sure to allow a little time to enjoy the castle's **gardens,** planned in the mid-18th century by Lancelot "Capability" Brown, the famous landscape gardener who also redesigned the grounds of Blenheim Palace. The entrance to the gardens is across the oval to the right and then to your left, following the signs to the Peacock Garden. The conservatory houses the Warwick Vase, five and a half feet tall, found in 1770 near Hadrian's Villa at Tivoli, outside Rome. In front of the conservatory are lovely Venetian-style gardens. If you have the time and the inclination, you might enjoy a stroll through the castle's extensive **park,** with its fine trees and shrubs and a family of peacocks. If you take this walk, on the way back toward the castle you will skirt the edge of Ethelfleda's Mound, supposedly the site of the earliest 10th-century castle. Finally, before leaving the castle grounds, you might want to visit the dungeon beneath Caesar's Tower and the armory. Both are to the right of the double gateway through which you entered the inner courtyard.

Return to the Castle Lodge and make a right turn into **Mill Street,** a lovely street lined with picturesque half-timbered houses. As this street descends toward the river, you get an unusual view of Warwick Castle towering above. Return back up Mill Street and turn right into Banbury Road. To your left just before you come to the river is the lovely St. Nicholas Park with its colorful flower beds. The **Castle Bridge,** which crosses the Avon in front of you, dates from the late 18th century, and from here you have one of the finest views of Warwick Castle looming over the treetops.

Continue along Banbury Road to **Bridge End,** just a short distance to the right past the bridge. Bridge End, one of the loveliest streets in Warwick, is lined with numerous tiny stone and half-timbered houses. Above it all towers the huge bulk of the castle across the river. You almost feel as if you've been transported back in time to the 16th century and you can imagine Queen Elizabeth on horseback riding past houses just like these on her way to being received at the castle by the Earl of Warwick. Follow Bridge End, which curves in a semicircle and returns to Banbury Road. Turn left and walk back toward the town. To your right is Myton Road; a short distance off this road is Warwick School, one of the half dozen oldest schools in England, having been founded about 914, more than a hundred fifty years before the Norman Conquest. One of the school's foremost graduates was John Masefield, who served as Poet Laureate from 1930 until his death in 1967.

Cross the river again and walk along Banbury Road back to Castle Lodge. Across from the Lodge you see the church of **St. Nicholas,** whose present-day appearance dates from the end of the 18th century. This church occupies the site of an ancient Anglo-Saxon nunnery destroyed in the early 11th century by the invading Danes. Go inside for a moment to see the unique modern glass mosaic on the northeast side of the nave; it was dedicated recently, in 1968. This window is unusual in that large chunks of colored glass have been attached to plate-glass panels. The effect you get is of thickness and texture, rather than the delicacy characteristic of medieval stained glass windows.

Once more return to Castle Lodge and from here walk along Castle Hill toward the **East Gate.** This gate stands at the entrance to one of Warwick's main thoroughfares, Jury Street, and was once part of the medieval city walls which used to surround the city. The chapel which sits atop East Gate was built in the 15th century and has been part of the Kings High School for Girls since 1879. Adjoining East Gate on the right are two medieval cottages, and next door to them is **Landor House,** built in 1692. The Victorian poet and essayist William Savage Landor was born in this house in 1775. Landor House is also part of the Kings High School.

Turn around, walk past East Gate, and enter **Jury Street,** which is lined with 17th- and 18th-century houses. On your right is the Lord Leycester Hotel, occupying the site of what was once the country home of Robert Dudley, Earl of Leicester. Robert's brother, Ambrose, was once occupant of Warwick Castle, and this may explain Robert's partiality for this town. On your left, at No. 2, you pass Pageant House, built in the Georgian style of the late 18th century. Walk to the intersection of Jury Street, High Street, Church Street, and Castle Street; on this site was once located Warwick's medieval High Cross marking the intersection of the main east-west and north-south roads through the town. Close to the High Cross, on the corner of Jury Street and Castle Street, used to be the Cross Tavern, an Elizabethan inn, which was given to the city of Warwick in 1576 by the Earl of Leicester partly as an exchange for the buildings which were to become Lord Leycester's Hospital. On the site of this tavern you now see the Italianate-style **Court House,** built in 1725 by Francis Smith. Notice the colonnaded stone façade with the statue of Justice above the main entrance. Ask to see the upstairs assembly room.

Turn left at the corner and stroll down Castle Street. Many of its charming houses were built prior to 1694. These houses are unusual in Warwick, because in 1694 a devastating fire swept through the city, destroying a great part of St. Mary's and 200 of the city's houses. To your left are the pleasant Pageant Gardens, a delightful public park, if you wish to stop and rest for a few minutes. At the end of Castle Street, you see the **Oken House,** a small half-timbered dwelling, one of a group of Elizabethan houses. In the 16th century this was the home of Thomas Oken, who was a mercer (textile merchant), a bailiff, and one of Warwick's leading philanthropists. He died in 1573 and left his money for distribution among the town's poor. Today, four hundred years after his death, a feast is still held annually to honor the memory of Thomas Oken and his wife, Joan. The Oken home now houses a marvelous Doll Museum (hours: weekdays, 10–6; Sunday, 2:30–5) with a collection of over a thousand wooden, wax, and porcelain dolls, as well as some antique toys.

Return up Castle Street and turn left into **High Street,** which is also lined with attractive 17th- and 18th-century houses. You pass two fine old hotels, the Aylesford, built in 1696, and the Warwick Arms, a famous late-18th-century posting house. At the end of High Street is the 12th-century **West Gate,** which, like its twin East Gate at the end of Jury Street, was once part of the medieval wall encircling the city. On top of the gate sits the **Chapel of St. James,** built in 1123 and restored in 1863. It is now part of the Lord Leycester Hospital and is still used for services by the Hospital's brethren.

Just to the right of the West Gate is the splendid group of half-timbered buildings known as **Lord Leycester's Hospital.** In the 14th century these buildings housed three powerful religious guilds which virtually ran the town. The guilds were dissolved in the mid-16th century and the buildings converted into an asylum for twelve poor soldiers in 1571 by Robert Dudley. Four hundred years later, Lord Leycester's Hospital is still home to retired old soldiers, who, on state occasions, wear black gowns with the original silver badges of 1571. These gentlemen will guide you around the Hospital today if you like (hours: summer, 10–6; winter, 10–4). The buildings surround a lovely, quiet quadrangle, from which you can visit the Great Dining Hall in which James I was entertained by Fulke Greville in 1617, the Chaplain's Dining Hall (now a regimental museum of the Queen's Own Hussars), and the former Guild Hall, with the chair used by James I during the festivities of 1617.

Past West Gate, turn right into Bowling Green Street and then make a right into Market Street. In a few minutes you will be in Market Place, with the old **Market Hall** to your right. A market has been located on this site since the 14th century. In 1670, William Hurlbutt constructed the stone building you see before you today. The structure was built on open arches for easy access to the goods offered for sale. The first floor was used for everything from puppet shows to cockfights, and the attic was used as a debtors' prison. This building is now the Warwick County Museum (hours: weekdays, 10–12, 1–5:30; Sunday, 2:30–5), with exhibits on the geology, archeology, and natural history of Warwickshire.

From the museum, turn left, then left again into New Street. At the end of New Street, turn right into Old Square, and directly ahead of you rises the collegiate church of **St. Mary.** A church has existed on this site since before the Norman Conquest. In 1123, Roger, Earl of Warwick, began building the Norman structure which existed for almost six centuries until the great fire of 1694. The crypt, the choir, and the Beauchamp Chapel fortunately survived this fire, but the nave, transepts, and tower (which can be ascended) had to be rebuilt. Plans submitted by the famous 17th-century architect Sir Christopher Wren, who rebuilt many of London's churches after the great London fire of 1666, were rejected, and the task of rebuilding went instead to Sir William Wilson, whose design was a mixture of Gothic and Renaissance styles.

Inside (hours: summer, 10–7; winter, 10–4), walk down the spacious, well-lit nave toward the choir. This **choir,** in Perpendicular Gothic style, dates from the end of the 14th century, and is distinguished by its splendid groined roof. In the center of the choir rest Thomas Beauchamp, Earl of Warwick, and his wife, Katherine. Beauchamp, who died in 1369, was the companion and supporter of Prince Edward (called the Black Prince), eldest son of Edward III, at the battles of Crecy and Poitiers fought in France during the Hundred Years War. He also built Caesar's Tower, which you saw earlier on your visit to Warwick Castle, and initiated the building of this choir. Beneath the choir (entrance through the choir vestry to the left) you can visit the 12th-century **Norman crypt,** supported by huge, squat columns. Here you see part of an ancient ducking stool, one of only two such stools still in existence.

On the north side of the vestry is the mid-14th-century **Chapter House.** Although St. Mary's was never a cathedral church, it did possess a chapter of canons and they used to assemble here. You can see the huge tomb of Fulke Greville, Lord Brooke, who was killed by one of his servants in 1628. He was both a poet and a statesman, and served as advisor to both Elizabeth I and her Stuart successor, James I. James gave Warwick Castle to Greville in 1604 and made him Lord Brooke seventeen years later. The inscription on Greville's tomb summarizes his long life: SERVANT TO QUEENE ELIZABETH, CONCELLER TO KING JAMES, AND FREND TO SIR PHILLIP SYDNEY.

Now walk to the right of the choir to see the highlight of St. Mary's, the **Beauchamp Chapel.** Just outside the entrance to the chapel, on the right wall, is a memorial to the second Thomas Beauchamp, also Earl of Warwick, who died in 1401. He was imprisoned in the Tower of London in 1397 because of his opposition to Richard II. The bear is part of the emblem of the Earls of Warwick and the oath which Richard swore at the time, "I cannot muzzle you but I will muzzle your bear," explains the muzzled bear on the family emblem (see the chapel entrance)— although, oddly enough, the bear on the memorial has no muzzle. Thomas Beauchamp was released upon Richard's death and the accession of Henry IV in 1399. Go into the magnificent Beauchamp Chapel, one of the finest examples of 15th-century Perpendicular Gothic style in England. Note the frequent use of the bear and ragged staff, the emblem of the Earls of Warwick. The stained glass, the stalls, and the fresco of the Last Judgment above the west door all date from the mid-15th century. In the center of the chapel is the marble **tomb of Richard Beauchamp,** who died in 1439. The bronze effigy of this earl is surrounded by fourteen statuettes of mourners. Richard Beauchamp was one of Henry V's chief counselors and the guardian of Henry VI, who was an infant at his father's death. Beauchamp was also governor of Rouen at the time of Joan of Arc's burning in 1431 (and the chief inquisitor at her trial). He died in Rouen eight years after Joan's death. On the north side of the chapel is the painted monument of Robert Dudley and his third wife, Lettice Knollys. Dudley died in 1588, and Lettice survived her husband by forty-six years. On the opposite side is the tomb of Dudley's son, Robert, called the "noble impe," who died at the age of three. Ambrose Dudley, Robert's brother, the Earl of Warwick, also rests in this chapel. Between the Beauchamp Chapel and the choir, be sure to stop at the exquisite little chantry with the elaborate fan vaulting.

Before leaving St. Mary's, see the memorial to William Landor at the west end. He was born in Warwick near the East Gate in 1775. Leave St. Mary's and turn right, walking along Northgate Street, which is lined with 18th-century houses. Across the street from St. Mary's is **Shire Hall.** Between 1676 and 1686, a building was erected on this site, where courts had been held for the preceding two hundred years by William Hurlbutt, who also built the Market Hall you visited earlier. Hurl-butt's building was replaced in 1753 by the classical building you see today, which contains a main hall, two law courts, and a grand-jury room. See if you can find the keeper and go inside to see the fine wooden-coffered and stucco ceilings.

Continue up Northgate Street and turn right along Priory Road. On the left side of this street is the large public park called Priory Park. An ancient ecclesiastical establishment founded by Henry de Newburgh, Earl of Warwick in the time of Henry I, once existed here. This monastery disappeared to make way for a mansion in the reign of Elizabeth I. Finally, the mansion was purchased and shipped to America stone by stone and the site became a park. Bear right down Chapel Street to Smith Street, where medieval armorers used to have their forges.

Smith Street leads to St. John's Street. On your right you come to the lovely 17th-century building called **St. John's,** which occupies the site of a 12th-century medieval hospital founded by Henry de Newburgh during the reign of Henry II. About 1620, the Stoughton family built their mansion here; from the late 18th to the early 20th century, a private boarding school occupied the mansion. Walk through the elaborate wrought-iron entrance gates, added in 1700, to visit the two museums now housed in the mansion. On the ground floor, you can examine furniture, folk crafts, and costumes, part of the Warwick County Museum collection, and on the first floor you'll find a regimental museum (hours for the Warwick County Museum collection: weekdays, excluding Tuesday, 10–12:30, 1:30–5:30; Sunday, from May to September, 2:30–5; hours for the regimental museum: Monday, Wednesday, and Thursday, 10–4:30; Friday, 10–4; Saturday, 1:30–5:30; closed Tuesday and Sunday). Before you leave, be sure to take a short stroll through the mansion's English Jacobean garden, where your walk through this charming city comes to an end.

*   *   *

One excursion you must make while visiting Warwick is to the ruins of one of England's greatest baronial castles, **Kenilworth.** Kenilworth was once the home of Robert Dudley, Earl of Leicester, and the site of Sir Walter Scott's early-19th-century romance of the same name. Leave Warwick by Coventry Road,

A429 (which begins at the intersection of St. John's Street and Coten End), which runs north. After five miles you will reach Kenilworth Castle.

This magnificent ruin in its poetic setting has a long and interesting history. Kenilworth was built in the early 12th century by Geoffrey de Clinton, treasurer to Henry I. In its early years it was visited by Henry II, John, and Henry III, and possession of the castle for centuries wavered between the House of Lancaster and the Crown. In 1362, John of Gaunt, son of Edward III and father of Henry IV, acquired the castle by marriage and greatly expanded it by adding the Banqueting Hall, the White Hall, and the Strong Tower. Two hundred years later, Elizabeth I gave Kenilworth to her favorite, Robert Dudley. He too enlarged the castle, adding "Leicester's Buildings." Dudley regally entertained his queen four times at Kenilworth, and the revelries on these royal visits are vividly described in Scott's novel. In 1611, the castle once again reverted to the Crown. The ruins you see before you today were caused by Oliver Cromwell's officers during the Great Civil War. Sir Walter Scott based his romance *Kenilworth* on the events surrounding the secret marriage of Amy Robsart to Robert Dudley, and a substantial portion of his action takes place at Kenilworth during one of Elizabeth's visits. Of course, most of the novel is imaginary: Amy Robsart died mysteriously in 1560, three years before Kenilworth was even given to Robert Dudley.

Today, as you wander about the remains of Kenilworth Castle (hours: April, weekdays and Sunday, 9:30–5:30; May to September, weekdays and Sunday, 9:30–7; March and October, weekdays, 9:30–5:30; Sunday, 2–5:30; November to February, weekdays, 9:30–4; Sunday, 2–4), you need a little of Scott's imagination to picture the castle as it must have been four hundred years ago when Elizabeth visited it. The only part of Kenilworth still habitable is Leicester's Gatehouse, built in 1570, and this is now a private residence. You can visit the 12th-century Norman keep called Caesar's Tower and the 14th-century Strong Tower, added by John of Gaunt, which Scott called "Mervyn's Tower" and where Amy Robsart supposedly stayed. You can also see the remains of John of Gaunt's great Banqueting Hall and Robert Dudley's 16th-century addition which housed Elizabeth in 1575.

WINCHESTER

Winchester is the city of kings, bishops, and scholars; all contributed to the greatness and importance which the city enjoyed for over a thousand years. The kings made Winchester their capital, building castles and palaces for themselves. The bishops made Winchester one of the most important episcopal cities in England, endowing it first with a Norman cathedral and later with a magnificent Gothic edifice. The scholars—and they included both kings and bishops—made Winchester a center of learning both in Anglo-Saxon times and in the Middle Ages, when Winchester College became the focal point of scholarship. All these people succeeded in making Winchester preeminent among English cities in splendor, beauty, and scholarly achievement.

Winchester's history goes back to the centuries before Christ, when native British tribes settled alongside the River Itchen. The Romans came in the middle of the first century, renamed the settlement Venta Belgarum, and stayed for 350 years. The Saxons followed the Romans, called the city Wintanceaster, and made it their capital in the early 6th century. From the 6th century until the 12th, Winchester reigned supreme among English cities. Egbert, king of Wessex, who was acknowledged king of England in 827, made Winchester his capital, as did successive Saxon kings. The Danes overran southern England in the 11th century; they too chose Winchester as their capital. Their chief, Canute, succeeded not only in conquering Winchester but also in winning the affections of his Saxon predecessor's wife. The Normans came in 1066, and their leader too, William the Conqueror, made Winchester his capital, although he was shrewd enough to make London his "other" capital, and was crowned king in both cities. A century after the Conquest, Winchester, after 600 years at the center of English life, began to lose its privileged status to this other thriving and rapidly growing capital. Although royal influence over Winchester decreased during the Middle Ages, English monarchs returned to their former capital to be married, to have their heirs born here, or to build their royal residences.

At about the same time the kings abandoned Winchester in favor of London, the city began to grow in ecclesiastical importance. A Norman cathedral was built shortly after the Conquest. This edifice was transformed in the 14th century by two Winchester bishops with vision, foresight, and a love of beauty. The area adjacent to the cathedral, called The Close, began to be filled with a variety of interesting medieval buildings, all part of a Benedictine monastery which flourished until the 16th century when Henry VIII dissolved English abbeys and monasteries. While the cathedral was being built, William of Wykeham founded Winchester College, which quickly became the model for the great public-school system in England.

Winchester's greatness suffered a severe decline during the Interregnum under Oliver Cromwell and after the Restoration. Charles II started to build a new royal palace to replace the one destroyed by Cromwell's armies, but it was incomplete at his death, and his successors neglected it. The cathedral also suffered greatly from the "zeal" of Cromwell's Puritans, and lost many of its treasures. Since the late 17th century, Winchester has remained relatively quiet and remote, more a spectator than an actor.

As you stroll through this ancient city today, you will see much that its past kings, bishops, and scholars have left behind—the remains of a once great castle, the superb cathedral and its peaceful Close, the medieval college. You will also walk along streets which were once major Roman roads, past medieval almshouses, Elizabethan half-timbered houses, and Georgian mansions. Winchester is a rich city, fortunate to have retained so much of its ancient heritage and so much of its beauty.

Begin your stroll through the ancient capital city of Winchester at the east end of High Street just beneath the huge bronze **statue of King Alfred.** This statue was set up in 1901 to commemorate the 9th-century king whom many consider the founder of the English nation. Over one thousand years ago, Alfred not only made Winchester his capital, but also gathered scholars here to make it a center of learning. Behind King

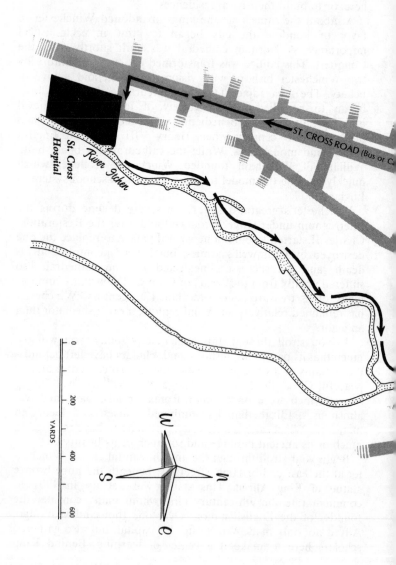

St. Cross Hospital

River Itchen

ST. CROSS ROAD (Bus or Ca

0   200   400   600
YARDS

N W S E

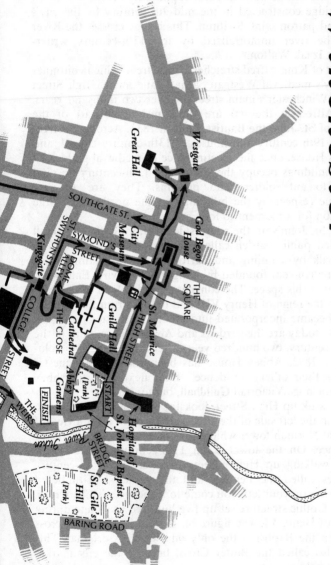

Winchester

Great Hall

Westgate

God Begot House

THE SQUARE

SOUTHGATE ST.

City Museum

ST. SWITHUN ST.

SYMOND'S STREET

DOME ALLEY

St. Maurice

Kingsgate

COLLEGE STREET

THE CLOSE

Cathedral

Abbey Gardens

Guild Hall

HIGH STREET

START

THE WEIRS

Cathedral Gardens

FINISH

River Itchen

BRIDGE STREET

St. Gile's

Hospital of St. John the Baptist

Hill (Park)

St. Gile's (Park)

BARING ROAD

Alfred is the bridge built in 1813, supposedly on the site of an earlier bridge constructed in the mid-9th century by the city's bishop and patron saint, Swithun. This bridge crosses the River Itchen, the river immortalized by the 17th-century writer-fisherman Izaak Walton.

In front of King Alfred stretches High Street, which continues to the city's medieval Westgate, a half mile away. High Street has been Winchester's main street for over two thousand years. Behind Alfred to the left are the almshouses, part of the **Hospital of St. John the Baptist,** built in 1833. Across the street are more 19th-century almshouses, a 13th-century chapel, and St. John's House, once the meetingplace of medieval guilds. All of these buildings occupy the site of the 13th-century hospital founded to aid soldiers and pilgrims. They are all very picturesque (especially the buildings on the north side of the street). Stop for a moment to look around.

Behind St. John's on the south side of High Street is a small flower-filled public garden called **Abbey Gardens,** set off from the sidewalk by a railing and narrow moat. Nunnaminster, a Benedictine convent founded by King Alfred's wife, Eahlswith, once covered this space. The convent was dissolved in the 16th century in the reign of Henry VIII and fell into ruins. Gradually its stone became incorporated into other Winchester buildings. On the site today are the gardens and **Abbey House,** built in the mid-18th century, two hundred years after the convent's dissolution. Since 1892, Abbey House has been used by Winchester mayors as their official residence. Right next door to Abbey House is the huge Victorian **Guildhall,** built in 1873.

As you walk up High Street, look for a passageway with two columns on the left side of the street. Go through it for a view of the ancient Norman tower which was once part of the church of St. Maurice. On the tower is an 11th-century sundial. Now continue walking up High Street. Just past the 16th-century colonnades called the Pentice, and the gabled half-timbered Tudor houses on your left, you come to Winchester's **City Cross,** an ornate Gothic structure set up five hundred years ago during the reign of Henry VI. The figure on the south side of the cross of St. John the Baptist is the only one which is original. This cross is also called the Butter Cross, because the city market used to be held at its base.

Just beyond the cross is the **Old Guildhall,** which now houses a branch of Lloyd's Bank. Notice the unique clock, erected in 1713 to commemorate the signing of the Treaty of Utrecht, ending the war with France. This was the war in which John Churchill, first Duke of Marlborough, distinguished himself. The statue of Queen Anne, next to the clock, was donated by two early-18th-century members of Parliament; Queen Anne was the reigning monarch at the time of the signing of the Treaty. If you cross the street, you can see the squat bell tower above the Old Guildhall. Known as the Curfew Belltower, it has rung the 8 P.M. curfew for centuries.

Across the street is the Tudor house called the **God Begot House.** This 16th-century house occupies the site of an ancient manor house which was given to Queen Emma upon her marriage to the Saxon King Ethelred the Unready in the early part of the 11th century. Emma later gave her manor house to the cathedral. Although the half-timbering on the front of God Begot is modern, you can see the timbering as it looked four hundred years ago if you go around to the back of the house via the Royal Oak Passage to the left. This passageway once marked the eastern boundary of the Jewish ghetto. The Jews were expelled from England in 1290, during the reign of Edward I. In this same passageway you pass the Royal Oak Tavern, established in 1630, which claims to be the oldest pub in England. You might consider stopping off here later on for a typical English kidney pie and a pint of ale.

Continue around the back of the God Begot House to St. Peter Street and turn left. The elegantly simple house at No. 4 was built in the late 17th century for the Duchess of Portsmouth, a favorite of that ladies' man Charles II. A little farther along St. Peter Street, on the same side of the street, you come to the lovely 18th-century **Avebury House,** owned in the 19th century by one of Winchester's leading families, the Mayos.

Return to High Street and the City Cross. Behind the cross is a passageway leading to the little shopping precinct known as **The Square.** Just under the arcade, to your left, is the 15th-century **Church of St. Lawrence.** It is believed that William the Conqueror, the first of the Norman kings, built his royal palace in the vicinity of The Square, and St. Lawrence's occupies the site of the Conqueror's 11th-century Chapel Royal. Since 1662, when Bishop Morley became bishop of Winchester, it has become the tradition for Winchester bishops-to-be to robe here before marching in procession to the cathedral for their installation. The church's rectory, located in The Square around the corner to your left, now houses the Eclipse Inn.

Across The Square, you can visit Winchester's **City Museum** (hours: May to August, Monday to Saturday, 10–6; in March, April, September, and October, the museum closes at 5; from November to February, at 4; Sunday, year-round, 2–4:30; closed holidays). The museum contains displays from all eras of Winchester's long history and includes pre-Christian Belgic pottery, Roman frescoes and mosaics, Saxon ornaments, medieval stonework, and 18th- and 19th-century artifacts. Be sure to see the lovely mosaic floor found in a nearby Roman villa; it's on the top floor of the museum.

From The Square, walk along **Great Minster Street,** one of the loveliest of the many picturesque streets in Winchester. It is lined with charming early-19th-century houses and shops. At the end of Great Minster, to your left, looms one of the most beautiful and best-known of all English cathedrals, **Winchester Cathedral.** Thirty-five English kings were crowned here, twenty lie buried here, and it is a monument to the first English monarchs. In the early 7th century, St. Birinus proselytized throughout southern England, and succeeded in converting the Wessex king, Cynegils. Two hundred years later, King Alfred the Great ordered an abbey built adjoining the Old Minster. This abbey, known as the New Minster, was completed in the early years of the 10th century. Recent excavations on the north side of the present cathedral have revealed the sites of both the Old and New Minsters. But in the year 1079, just thirteen years after the Norman Conquest, the Norman bishop, Walkelin, began construction of a new cathedral.

Walk toward the cathedral along the avenue of trees first planted in the 17th century. The great **west window** before you contains fragments of the original 14th-century stained glass; this window as well as others in the church suffered severe damage during the Civil War of 1642, when Puritan zealots rampaged through the cathedral, destroying and mutilating. Enter the cathedral through the west doorway. Before you is one of the most beautiful of all English cathedrals, a compendium of architectural styles spanning four centuries, from the cathedral's consecration at the end of the 11th century to the Dissolution in the early 16th century during the reign of Henry VIII. The plan of the cathedral is Bishop Walkelin's, but only the transepts retain the original Norman style, which once characterized the entire 11th-century structure. Bishop Godfrey de Lucy added the retrochoir at the east end of the church at the end of the 12th century; it is Early English Gothic in style. Two centuries later, Bishops William of Edington and William of Wykeham transformed the Norman nave into the late Gothic style, called English Perpendicular, which you see before you today.

The **nave,** the second longest in Europe (after St. Peter's in Rome), was originally sturdy Norman work with thick walls, massive pillars, and a flat roof. Bishops Edington and Wykeham enclosed the Norman pillars in Gothic-style shells and replaced the flat roof in the late 14th century. Walk down the center of the nave to the lovely **chantry,** one of seven such chantries in the church, designed by Bishop William of Wykeham to hold his tomb. He was not a man who rested merely on his laurels as bishop of a major cathedral. He was also Lord Chancellor to both Edward III and Richard II, and founded New College at Oxford and, a few years later, Winchester College, which you will visit a little later. Inside the chantry is the splendid painted effigy of the bishop, who died in 1404. Notice the three monks sitting at his feet.

Opposite Bishop Wykeham's chantry, in the north aisle, are a **brass tablet** and a stained glass window commemorating Jane Austen, who died in Winchester in 1817. She rests beneath the pavement in front of the window. If you have time while in Winchester you might want to make a "pilgrimage" to Chawton, only seventeen miles away, to see where Jane Austen spent the last nine years of her life writing *Emma, Mansfield Park,* and *Persuasion.* Close to her memorial is the mid-12th-century **baptismal font,** a gift of Bishop Henry de Blois, carved with legends from the life of St. Nicholas. It is made of black Flemish marble, and there are only eight like it in all of England.

On the right, as you approach the choir, is the chantry containing the alabaster figure of Bishop William of Edington, who died in 1366. Bishop Edington was yet another Winchester bishop who served also as Lord Chancellor of England. Walk to the right of Bishop Edington into the **south transept,** which remains the same as the day it was completed, almost nine hundred years ago. In the center is the elaborate memorial of Bishop Samuel Wilberforce, who died in 1873. Behind the bishop, the chapel to the left was built by Prior Silkestede in the early 16th century. Here you see the magnificent **stained glass window** erected by fishermen from all over the world as a memorial to Izaak Walton, the 17th-century author of *The Compleat Angler.* Walton, who died in 1683, spent the last twenty years of his life in Winchester; his name is inextricably linked with Winchester's River Itchen. Note the figure of Walton in the lower right and lower left of the window, with fishing scenes from the New Testament in between. From this south transept is an entrance to the **Cathedral Library,** where you can see a 10th-century copy of the Venerable Bede's *Ecclesiastical History* and a 12th-century illuminated bible.

Turn right from the south transept and walk through the 13th-century **Pilgrim's Gate,** which separates the south transept from the retrochoir. This gate was once used to keep pilgrims visiting the shrine of St. Swithun in the retrochoir from interfering with other church services. You immediately notice the outward leaning of the walls. In the early years of this century, it was discovered that the south side of the cathedral was sinking in watery soil; with much effort, ingenuity, and money, the south wall was successfully underpinned and steel bars connect outer walls to inner columns.

On your way into the retrochoir on the left is the Gothic chantry of Bishop Richard Fox, founder of Corpus Christi College, Oxford, who died in 1528. The **retrochoir** is the part of the church enlarged by Bishop de Lucy to accommodate the hordes of pilgrims visiting the shrine of Winchester's 9th-century bishop, St. Swithun. In the center of the retrochoir you can see the modern **shrine of St. Swithun,** erected in 1962; the previous shrine was despoiled in 1538 during the Dissolution of the abbeys and monasteries. In front of this shrine is the plain tomb of the retrochoir's builder, Godfrey de Lucy, who died in 1204.

The elaborate chantry to the right of St. Swithun's shrine (as you face east) is that of **Cardinal Henry de Beaufort,** Henry IV's brother. The cardinal, who died in 1447, is stigmatized as the chief judge presiding over the heresy trial of Joan of Arc, and surely it is intentional irony that her statue should be just a few feet away. Next to St. Swithun on the left is **Bishop William of Waynflete's chantry.** Bishop Waynflete was another Winchester prelate who was not content to simply administer his bishopric. He was also headmaster of Winchester College, founder of Magdalen College, Oxford, and first provost of Eton. He died in 1486.

In the left corner of the retrochoir is the late-12th-century **Guardian Angels Chapel,** with lovely 13th-century roof medallions, and the 17th-century tomb of Sir Richard Weston, Earl of Portland. As you leave the retrochoir by the north side, see **Bishop Stephen Gardiner's chantry** on the left. Bishop Gardiner died in 1555, a year after conducting the marriage ceremony of Queen Mary Tudor and Philip II of Spain. The chair Mary sat on during the ceremony is preserved in this chantry. Supposedly, it was a papal wedding gift. Mary is known as "Bloody Mary" for her attempt to forcibly return England to Roman Catholicism.

Just past the chantry, turn left into the **presbytery** (the east end of the choir), which is enclosed by delicate filigreelike stone screens. Atop these screens are six painted **mortuary chests** bearing the bones of many early English monarchs, including Cynegils, who built the Old Minster, Egbert, acknowledged as the first king of all England in the early 9th century, Ethelwulf, and Canute, the first Danish king of England, with his wife, Emma. Emma is unique in English history: She was not only Canute's spouse but also the wife of his predecessor Ethelred the Unready, the mother of two English kings, Hardicanute and Edward the Confessor, and stepmother of two more, Edmund Ironside and Harold I. The **reredos** or altar screen at the east end of the presbytery is an ornate piece of 15th-century workmanship. During the Reformation, the statues were mutilated or destroyed; those you see today were placed here at the end of the last century.

Behind you is the **choir,** separated from the nave by an oak screen. The 60 oak **choir stalls** and misericords, dating from 1308, are among the oldest and most beautiful in England. The **pulpit** was given to the cathedral in 1520 by Prior Thomas of Silkestede. The marble tomb in the middle of the choir, beneath the transept crossing, is said to contain the bones of William

Rufus, the Conqueror's son and successor, who died in 1100. Seven years after his death, the cathedral's bell tower came crashing down, and Winchester citizens interpreted the collapse as an omen that William Rufus, an acknowledged heretic, should never have been buried in the cathedral. However, here he still rests. The tower has been rebuilt, although it is now only a squat 138 feet high (compared, for instance, to Salisbury's, which is 404 feet).

From the choir, walk to the **north transept,** also substantially unchanged from its original Norman style. To the left at the bottom of the stairs is the small 12th-century **Holy Sepulchre Chapel,** with 13th-century frescoes of Christ's Passion and Death. On the west side of this transept, in the **Epiphany Chapel,** are four stained glass windows by the 19th-century pre-Raphaelite artists Sir Edward Burne-Jones and William Morris. Also in this north transept is the entrance to the **crypt,** which can be visited only in dry months. During much of the year, the crypt is often flooded, sometimes to a depth of three feet, due to the marsh in which the cathedral stands.

Cross the nave and leave the cathedral by its south door, which once led to the cloisters destroyed in the reign of Elizabeth I. To your left you see the Norman arcade adjoining the south transept; the arcade is all that remains of the chapter house which once stood here. Next to the arcade is the **Deanery,** partially 13th century, with a red brick 17th-century addition built for Charles II while his Winchester palace was being constructed (behind the part of the building you see—walk around to the left). The part of the cathedral grounds in which the Deanery is situated is called **The Close,** and was once surrounded by the medieval buildings of St. Swithun's Priory, the Benedictine monastery which serviced the cathedral. Now there are remains of the ancient monastery walls and a beautiful assortment of medieval, Tudor, and 17th-century houses. The Deanery is one such example. To your left is **Dome Alley,** lined on both sides by lovely mid-17th-century houses. Izaak Walton died in the house at No. 7, the home of his son-in-law, Dr. Hawkins, a canon of the cathedral. Return to the Deanery. Close by are the 14th-century **Pilgrim's Hall,** with a hammer-beam ceiling, the 17th-century **Pilgrim's School,** and the picturesque 16th-century **Priory Stables.**

Next walk through the **Kingsgate,** one of two medieval gates surviving in the city, into College Street and turn left. This street, one of the prettiest in the city, is lined with houses of the 17th and 18th centuries. Jane Austen lived in the house at No. 8 while working on her last novel, *Persuasion.* She had come to Winchester from Chawton to be near her doctor, and she died in this house in July 1817, at the age of 41. Just beyond is **Winchester College,** founded by Bishop William of Wykeham in 1382 and allied with New College at Oxford, which Bishop Wykeham had founded three years prior. This college, the oldest among the great English schools, was to become the model for the English public-school system. At first the college had only 70 scholars, who passed on to Oxford upon graduation. Today there are still 70 scholars occupying the quarters their predecessors inhabited 600 years ago, but there are also 450 other students in attendance. Among the most famous of the college's graduates were William Grocyn, Anthony Trollope, Dr. Thomas Arnold and his son, Matthew, and William Collins.

You will visit the college in a few moments. For now, continue along College Street. Across the street, enclosed by a portion of the old City Wall are the ruins of **Wolvesey Castle.** Begun in 1129, by Bishop Henry de Blois, half brother of King Stephen and grandson of William the Conqueror, this fortress-palace was destroyed 500 years later in 1646 by Oliver Cromwell's armies. Only fragments of the original buildings remain, but restoration is in progress. Adjacent to the ruins is **Wolvesey Palace,** designed in 1674 by Christopher Wren as Bishop Morley's episcopal residence. Wren was working in Winchester at the time, on Charles II's new royal palace, which was to be erected on the site of the ancient Winchester Castle.

If you were to continue walking along College Street alongside the City Walls, you would come to **The Weirs,** a pleasant walk along the river, which would lead you back to High Street. Return, however, to Winchester College, and enter through the late-14th-century **Great Gateway** (hours: summer, Monday to Saturday, 10–6; Sunday, 2–6; it closes two hours earlier in winter), with its statue of the Virgin and Child. Although you can wander about through the courtyards and cloisters on your own when the college is open, to see areas normally closed to visitors you must join a guided tour (tours at 10, 11:45, 2, and 3 every day except Sunday morning; from April to September, there is an additional tour at 4:30). From the porter's lodge, you pass through the Outer Court into **Chamber Court,** which has been the center of the college's life for almost six hundred years. Around this courtyard are the rooms of Winchester College's seventy scholars. Directly ahead is the **chapel,** built in 1395, which still retains its original colorfully painted wooden fan-tracery ceiling and choir stalls. You will see the 15th-century reredos and the great east window, with the figures of the chapel's building crew beneath the head of the recumbent Jesse. At the southwest end of the chapel is Warden Thurburn's chantry, built in 1480. The stained glass window here depicts the kneeling figure of Richard II in the lower right corner and William of Wykeham in the lower left.

After visiting other parts of the college, you will be shown Bishop Wykeham's **cloister,** with John Fromond's 15th-century chapel in the middle, probably the only chapel in England so situated. John Fromond, who died in 1420, was steward of the manors owned by Winchester College. Nearby is the elegant brick building called the **School,** designed by Christopher Wren in 1683. Above the doorway is a statue of the college's founder, Bishop Wykeham. Inside, on one wall, is the famous Latin Wykehamite (as graduates of the college are called) motto, which translates as "Either learn or leave, or stay for a third choice—to be licked." Before leaving the college, be sure to visit the **War Memorial Cloister,** built in 1924 by Sir Herbert Baker to commemorate the dead of World War I. Beyond the War Memorial stretch the college's meadows and cricket fields.

Leave the college grounds by the War Memorial gateway and you are in Kingsgate Street, another lovely street lined with 17th- and 18th-century houses. The house at No. 8 was built for the Duke of Buckingham when Charles II resided in the city. Return to Kingsgate and go beneath the arch. Turn left into St. Swithun Street, where, at No. 26/27, you see another Wren house (Wren was very busy in Winchester), this one built for Charles II's brother, the Duke of York, who later became James II. Return to Symond's Street. At the corner of St. Swithun Street and Symond's Street is Christes Hospital, an almshouse built in 1607 for a small number of unmarried men and young boys.

Turn left to walk along Symond's Street and then on Great Minster Street past The Square into High Street. Make a left and walk toward the Westgate. At No. 57 note the handsome façade of the building housing the Hampshire *Chronicle,* which has been publishing news for over two hundred years. Directly in front of you is the **Westgate,** one of the original five medieval gateways which led into Winchester; only this one and Kingsgate survive. The archway itself dates from the 13th century although the upper portion is a century later. This upper portion now houses a small **museum** (hours are the same as for the City Museum) illustrating the civic history of Winchester. You can see a unique collection of weights and measures, as well as the usual assortment of swords and armor. The museum once served as a prison, and two of its best-known inmates were Charles I and Sir Walter Raleigh. From the roof of the Westgate you have a view overlooking the city.

From the façade of the Westgate, facing away from High Street, turn left and walk to the **Great Hall** (hours: April to September, Monday to Friday, 10–5; October to March, Monday to Friday, 10–4), all that is left of Winchester Castle. On this site there was once a castle begun by William the Conqueror, enlarged by Henry III between 1222 and 1236, and altered by Richard II late in the 14th century. Henry III, son of King John, was born here in 1207, and so was Henry VII's oldest son, Arthur, in 1486. Arthur was Henry VIII's brother, and the first husband of Catherine of Aragon. Richard the Lion-Hearted returned here to live after his imprisonment in Austria following the Third Crusade. James I came here in 1603 to escape the plague in London. In 1645, Oliver Cromwell's armies completely destroyed the buildings, leaving only the Great Hall intact—Winchester's punishment for remaining loyal to Charles I. After the restoration of the monarchy in 1660, Charles II commissioned Christopher Wren in 1683 to build him a new royal palace on this site. Work continued throughout the reign of Charles II and his successors, but ceased at the death of Queen Anne in 1714. The incomplete palace burned down in 1894.

The Great Hall itself dates from about 1235 and has witnessed many important events in English history. The first English parliaments met here; Sir Walter Raleigh, the greatest of

Elizabethan adventurers, and a favorite of Elizabeth I, was tried and condemned to death in this hall in 1603 for conspiracy against Elizabeth's successor, James I; and in 1685 the infamous Judge George Jeffreys sentenced 320 people to death in a series of trials known as the "Bloody Assizes" after the unsuccessful insurrection of the Duke of Monmouth against James II. At the west end of the hall, above the royal dais, hangs the famous **Roundtable,** which supposedly belonged to the legendary King Arthur. This 18-foot-in-diameter table is first mentioned in the early 15th century and is referred to then as being very ancient. It would have to be old if it ever belonged to Arthur, who is supposed to have lived about the year 500. Painted in 1522 for the visit of Emperor Charles I, the table shows Arthur sitting dressed in Tudor robes with the red-and-white Tudor rose representing the merging of the Houses of York and Lancaster in the center. Around the edge of the table appear the names of Arthur's 24 knights of the round table. Indeed, the huge table you see before you today is capable of seating 25 people fairly comfortably.

Return to High Street and take the second right, Southgate Street, which has largely retained its 18th-century appearance. Along this street on the right is Serle's House. Originally constructed in 1715, it belonged to one of Winchester's leading families. In the last century, Peter Serle, a colonel in the South Hampshire Militia, gave the house to the city, and it now houses the **Royal Hampshire Regiment Museum.** Go inside (hours: Monday to Friday, 10–12:30, 2–4; closed holidays) to see an assortment of regimental uniforms, medals, and weapons.

To visit the oldest functioning almshouse in England, **St. Cross Hospital,** you can hire a cab or take one of the buses running along Southgate Street (make sure to ask if it goes to St. Cross; No. 47 is one that does)—or you can walk. It's only about a mile from Serle's House, and you can't get lost. Continue down Southgate Street, which becomes St. Cross Road. Turn left just before the Bell Inn. Founded by Bishop Henry de Blois in 1136 for thirteen poor and infirm men, the hospital was enlarged three hundred years later by Cardinal Henry de Beaufort. As you walk around the grounds of the hospital today, you will see elderly men dressed in black or claret-colored gowns. Those in black with a silver shield over the chest are the "descendents" of Henry de Blois's original thirteen men, and those wearing the claret gowns with the cardinal's hats are Henry de Beaufort's men. For hundreds of years this hospital has sheltered such men. Even today, wayfarers (and aren't you one?) can ask at the porter's lodge for the dole of bread and ale which the hospital has freely dispensed for the asking for the past eight hundred years.

To visit the hospital buildings you must join a guided tour (hours: April to October, 9–12:30, 2–5; November to March, 10:30–12:30, 2–3:30). Through the Beaufort Gatehouse with the statue of the second founder in one of the niches above, you enter the inner quadrangle, where you will be shown the master's house, the 15th-century brethren's houses, the refectory and kitchen, and the **chapel.** The chapel, built in the late 12th century, is an outstanding example of transitional Norman architecture, although it contains reminders from succeeding centuries. The tower is 14th-century, the stained glass windows 15th-century, and the unique oak lectern 16th-century.

After visiting St. Cross, you can take the bus back to High Street, but if you've any energy left at all, it's much more pleasant to leave the Hospital, turn right until you come to the River Itchen, and follow the river through fields and meadows back to High Street and the statue of Alfred the Great. To your right as you walk you will see **St. Catherine's Hill.** The clump of trees crowning the summit was planted two hundred years ago to mark the site of a 12th-century chapel.

* * *

Before leaving Winchester, there is one short excursion you should try to make. It takes you across the River Itchen via Bridge Street to **St. Gile's Hill** (or, if you drive, via Bridge Street, Magdalen Hill, and Alresford Road, making the first right turn you can off Alresford Road to a road marked "Baring Road unadopted"). This hill was once the site of a famous annual medieval fair. Today from the summit of the hill you have a marvelous view over the city you've just walked through with the cathedral prominent in the foreground.

GERMANY

HEIDELBERG

Heidelberg is a fairy-tale city, a city of quaint streets, baroque mansions, and picturesque student inns. Its famous ruined castle nestled against a verdant hillside dominates the old city, keeping an eye on all its doings as it has for almost 800 years. Above all, Heidelberg is a city with a gay, romantic heart—a city forever young. To realize this all you have to do is to stroll along the Hauptstrasse in the evening when the inns are filled to bursting with students singing and drinking, or stroll along the peaceful Philosophenweg high above the city on the opposite side of the river, with the beauty of town and castle spread out before you. Heidelberg, with its long, rich history, is a timeless city. Enjoy it, stroll through it leisurely, savor it, and fall in love with it, as many have before you.

Heidelberg's history stretches back to the time before history was recorded, to a time when man as he is today did not yet exist. Seventy years ago, a jawbone was uncovered in a sand pit not too far from the city. Archeologists have ascribed this fragment to a manlike creature they've named Heidelberg Man, who lived near the banks of the Neckar half a million years ago. There are traces of an agricultural community going back four thousand years, and Celtic tribes built primitive stone defenses on the Heiligenberg across the river from the castle about 500 B.C. The Romans came through in the first century, fortifying the right bank of the Rhine River, and in the third century, the Alemanni, a Germanic tribe, overran and settled the area.

We know very little about the nine centuries between 300 and 1200, but from the mid-12th century on, Heidelberg's history becomes the history of its castle. In 1155, Holy Roman Emperor Frederick Barbarossa named his stepbrother, Konrad of Hohenstaufen, Count Palatine of the Rhine. Seventy years later, Bishop Henry of Worms gave the castle-fortress already existing in Heidelberg to Ludwig I von Wittelsbach. A century later, Ludwig's descendent Rudolph I became Palatine Elector, one of seven princes who chose the Holy Roman Emperor from among

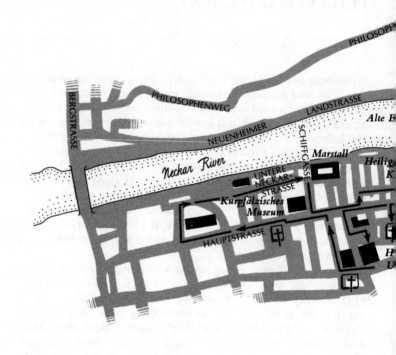

Heidelberg

0　　100　　200　　300
YARDS

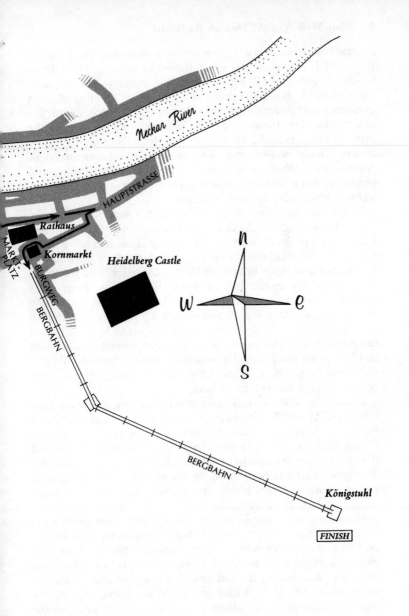

Neckar River

HAUPTSTRASSE

Rathaus

Kornmarkt

MARKT-PLATZ

BURGWEG

Heidelberg Castle

BERGBAHN

n

w   e

s

BERGBAHN

Königstuhl

FINISH

themselves. Heidelberg University was founded in 1386 by Ruprecht I. However, the great period of activity, Heidelberg Castle's "golden age," spanned the 16th century and the early years of the 17th century when five successive Palatine electors expanded and altered the castle. But hard on the heels of this prosperous period came disaster: Friedrich V, the last of the princely builders and a Protestant, left Heidelberg in 1619 to be crowned King of Bohemia. This act displeased Ferdinand of Austria, the Catholic contender for the Bohemian throne, and precipitated the devastation of the Thirty Years' War. Friedrich lost his crown, his city, and his castle.

Worse was to come. In 1671, Friedrich's son, Karl-Ludwig, married his daughter, Liselotte, to Philip d'Orleans, brother of France's Louis XIV. When Karl-Ludwig died without a male heir, Louis XIV laid claim to the Palatinate lands in the name of his brother and sister-in-law. In 1689, the French invaded, blew up much of the castle, and set fire to the old city. Four years later, they returned to complete the devastation, again setting fire to the city, which was almost completely reduced to ashes. In 1720, Elector Karl-Philip transferred the court to Mannheim, on the Rhine River, and Elector Karl-Theodor moved it to Munich in 1777, when the Palatinate and Bavaria were joined. In 1803, the territory to the east of the Rhine, including Heidelberg, became part of the Duchy of Baden.

During the 19th century, Heidelberg became a great tourist attraction. With its ruined castle, its picturesque situation, and its quaint old city, it attracted numerous painters and poets who rhapsodized its charms in paint or words. With the painters and the poets came the tourists who also fell in love with the city. This love affair has been going on for almost 200 years, and as you stroll around this lovely city today you too may become caught up in it. It's easy to do.

Heidelberg is an ideal city for walking, and since you'll want to stroll just a little more slowly in order to catch baroque details on buildings or to explore some picturesque little street on your own, you might want to divide this one busy day of sightseeing into two parts, seeing the old town on one day and saving the castle for another day. Whatever you decide, spend at least one night in Heidelberg to "carouse" in a student inn and see the castle by moonlight.

Begin your stroll through Heidelberg in the **Marktplatz** (Market Square). This is the city's main square, and if you're here on a Wednesday or a Saturday morning, you'll find it bustling with activity. The vendors' stalls are full of fresh flowers, fish, and vegetables. From here you have a marvelous view of the castle looming over the old city. Anywhere you walk in the city today, you will be very aware of this enormous castle's presence perched halfway up its green hillside.

Walk past the 18th-century Hercules fountain to Heidelberg's early-18th-century **Rathaus** (City Hall), housing a famous glockenspiel carillon. If you return to this spot at 7 P.M., you will hear a performance of folk melodies which includes the city's "theme song," "Alt Heidelberg, Du Feine" ("Old Heidelberg, You Fine One"), written by the city's poet laureate, Josef Viktor van Scheffel.

Opposite the Rathaus is the east end of the **Heiliggeist-Kirche** (Church of the Holy Ghost), the city's most important Protestant church. This large red sandstone building was erected almost six hundred years ago by Palatine-Elector Ruprecht III in flamboyant late Gothic style. Its 16th-century west tower, crowned by an octagonal belfry and a baroque spire, is the predominant landmark of the old city. As you walk along the south side of the church to the entrance, notice the tiny shops sheltered between the buttresses. Here they sell souvenirs and books in the same way that they sold religious articles five hundred years ago.

It is immediately evident as you enter that the interior of the Heiliggeist-Kirche is built in what is known as "hall style." The nave and the north and south aisles are exactly the same height, with pillars separating them. The effect of equal height is minimized by the galleries running above the north and south aisles. These galleries once housed the Bibliotheca Palatina, the Palatine Library, a magnificent collection of books gathered by Heidelberg's electors during the 15th and 16th centuries. The Library included the thousand manuscripts donated by wealthy Augsburg banker Ulrich Fugger in 1567. During the Thirty Years' War (1618–1648), Elector Maximilian of Bavaria defeated Heidelberg's Elector Friedrich V and conquered the city. Maximilian, a Catholic (Friedrich was a Protestant), sent the Bibliotheca Palatina to Rome in 1623 as his gift to the Pope. In 1815, some of the manuscripts were returned to Heidelberg, but the vast majority of the priceless collection is still part of the Pope's library.

Walk toward the well-lit choir; to the left is the simple, elegant **tomb of Elector Ruprecht III** (who died in 1410) and his wife, Elisabeth of Hohenzollern, with reclining effigies of the regal pair. Ruprecht was the builder of this church, and later became king. At one time, this choir held 54 tombs and monuments of electors and their consorts; from 1410 until 1685, the electors of the Palatinate were laid to rest here. In 1693, the French ravaged and burned the city and destroyed the tombs, but somehow Ruprecht's was the only one to escape this general destruction.

At first, the Heiliggeist-Kirche had been the church of the Catholics. But in the 16th century, with the advent of Protestantism, specifically Lutheranism, the church was taken over by these "dissenters" as their house of worship. Palatine-Elector Otto-Heinrich (1556–59) was the first of the Protestant electors. In 1706, it was decided that both Catholics and Protestants should be free to use the church, and a partition was set up dividing the choir from the nave. Catholics were given the choir, and Protestants the nave. The partition remained for 230 years, until 1936, when the Heiliggeist-Kirche became Heidelberg's Protestant parish church.

Leave the church by the Hauptstrasse exit. **Hauptstrasse** is Heidelberg's main street, and is lined with innumerable picturesque, ancient houses and taverns. One of the oldest and most interesting is directly across the street from the Heiliggeist-Kirche at No. 178 Hauptstrasse, the **Haus zum Ritter** (House of the Knight). This late-16th-century mansion, built as a private residence by a Belgian Huguenot cloth merchant, Charles Bélier, is regarded as the most handsome Renaissance building in the city. It is unique, as it is one of the very few buildings which remained undamaged after the great fire of 1693 which levelled most of the city. Note the erkers, or oriels, projections built out from the façade of a building to add space, admit light, and permit a view in three directions. The portraits of Charles Bélier and his spouse decorate the erker on the right, and on the left, appropriately enough, two rams are represented. The mansion, however, takes its name from the bust of St. George, arrayed in knightly armor, which crowns the pinnacle. Today, the Haus zum Ritter shelters and feeds weary sightseers as a hotel and restaurant.

Continue along Hauptstrasse for a few yards until you come to Kettengasse on your left. On the corner is Meder Haus, an ornate baroque mansion with a madonna in a niche on the corner. A little farther on is No. 160, where the 19th-century composer Robert Schumann lived while visiting Heidelberg in 1829–30. Just past this house, turn left into Heugasse (Hay Lane), a short street which leads you to Heidelberg's Catholic parish church, the **Jesuitenkirche** (Church of the Jesuits). This baroque church dates from the first half of the 18th century and was built by Johannes Adam Breunig, the architect responsible for many of Heidelberg's ornate 18th-century structures. Its slender mid-19th-century bell tower houses the oldest bell in the city, which is seven hundred years old. Before going inside, notice the statues of the two famous Jesuit saints on the façade. On the left is Ignatius Loyola, the founder of the Jesuit order, and on the right is Francis Xavier, its first missionary (to India and Japan). Step inside for a moment to see the typical hall church layout. The interior is lovely, with just the right touch of elegance and color (notice the chandeliers and the gilt-green at the tops of the pillars).

Return to Hauptstrasse and stroll along until you come to Grabengasse (Moat Lane) on the left. Grabengasse marked the city limits until 1392, and medieval ramparts once stood here. Walk past the fountain, topped by an imperial stone lion. You are in the midst of **Heidelberg University,** one of the most famous universities in the world. Founded in 1386 during the reign of Ruprecht I, this is Germany's oldest university, and there are now more than twelve thousand students (one out of ten people in Heidelberg). Much of its present-day fame rests on the reputation given it by Sigmund Romberg's 1924 operetta, *The Student Prince.* This lively operetta, set in the Heidelberg of the mid-19th century, revolves around young Prince Karl Franz, heir to the imaginary throne of Karlsberg, who comes incognito to study at the university. Of course, he promptly falls in love with the city, and with an innkeeper's lovely daughter as well. Unfortunately (and atypical of most love stories), the ending is not a happily-ever-after one: The prince must return to his kingdom to ascend the newly vacant throne and marry his predestined royal bride. Thousands who saw Romberg's operetta pictured Heidelberg as a fairy-tale city, its university filled with rambunctious, high-spirited students forever drinking and singing with a little dueling thrown in on the side for excitement.

On the left side is the **Alte Universität** (Old University), the oldest existing part of the university, built by Johannes Breunig in 1711. Earlier buildings were destroyed in the 1693 fire. Turn left into Universitätsplatz and then left again to No. 2 Augustinergasse, where you can visit the **Studentenkarzer** (Students' Prison). The jail (hours: every day, 9–5; November to February, closed on Sunday) consists of six rooms which were used from 1712 to 1914 to detain unruly students for varying periods of time: A student brought in drunk was sentenced to two weeks' imprisonment; dueling brought a four-weeks' sentence. Imprisonment here was not a stigma; rather, it became a mark of distinction, like being on an honor list. Nor was it a hardship: Jailed students were free to attend classes, and could go from room to room at night paying social calls on their incarcerated friends. Food was delivered from the student inns, and you can be sure that the singing and drinking that went on in the inns also went on here in the Studentenkarzer. Over the centuries, the walls and even the ceilings became filled with amusing graffiti and drawings, memorials to the many students who "served time" here.

Leave the Studentenkarzer and turn right to stroll along Augustinergasse. On the right you pass the **Neue Universität** (New University), which was built with money donated by Americans in the late 1920s. Jacob Schurman, U.S. Ambassador to Germany between 1925 and 1930, was once a student at Heidelberg University, and he collected the funds for building the Neue Universität. Continue straight ahead inside the courtyard to see the **Hexenturm** (Witch's Tower), a six-hundred-year-old tower which was part of the medieval fortifications along Grabengasse.

Walk up the steps to Seminarstrasse. Directly ahead is a huge baroque building called the **Collegium Academicum.** A Jesuit seminary in the mid-18th century, it has served the city of Heidelberg in a multitude of ways in the past two hundred years—as a school, an insane asylum, a hospital, barracks for soldiers, and, today, as a dormitory for university students.

Turn right along Seminarstrasse, cross Grabengasse, and to your left is **Peterskirche** (St. Peter's Church), the oldest parish church in the city, and now the church of Heidelberg University. A church existed on this site outside the walls of medieval Heidelberg as early as the 12th century, although the present Gothic church dates from the end of the 15th century. Stroll around the outside of the church, which for almost four hundred years served as a burial place for university professors and court officials. Notice the many memorials along the outside walls. Peterskirche is another example of the hall church style.

After leaving Peterskirche, cross the street to visit the baroque **Universitätsbibliothek** (University Library). In Room 109 this library (hours: weekdays, 11–12 only; closed Sunday and holidays) houses one of the jewels of medieval literature, a 14th-century illuminated manuscript called the Manessische manuscript. A unique collection of medieval lyrics, mostly love lyrics, it was written in the first half of the 14th century and decorated with 138 full-page miniature paintings. Even if you're not interested in medieval poetry, stop in for a few minutes to examine the exquisite, brightly colored paintings which accompany the lyrics.

From the entrance to the library, turn right, then right again to walk along Sandgasse to Hauptstrasse. Turn left and notice someone's fanciful recreation of a Roman archway at No. 110. No. 97 is Heidelberg's leading fine arts museum, **Kurpfälzisches Museum** (Palatinate Museum). The museum (hours: Tuesday to Sunday, 10–1, 2–5; closed Monday) occupies a large baroque mansion built in 1712 by Johannes Breunig for law professor Philip Morass. An interesting item is the lower jawbone of the famous **Heidelberg Man** in Room 49 (downstairs). It is estimated to date from about 500,000 B.C., and is the earliest evidence of man in Europe. The same room contains Roman and early Germanic antiquities from the first to the eighth century.

On the first floor are treasures from the Middle Ages and the Renaissance. In Room 30 is the masterpiece of this collection, the magnificently carved **Altarpiece of the Twelve Apostles**

(1509) by Tilman Riemenschneider of Würzburg, the greatest German sculptor of the Renaissance. Originally carved for the church of Windsheim, a tiny village near Rothenburg ob der Tauber, the altarpiece disappeared after the fire of 1730, which destroyed the church, and was presumed burned. In the last century, however, it was discovered here in the Kurpfälzisches Museum, covered with paint. How it got here, no one knows.

Also on this floor, near the stairs, is a room with Dutch and Flemish paintings of the 17th and 18th centuries, including those of Jan Breughel, Jan van Goyen, and several van Ruisdaels. Upstairs on the second floor is the museum's collection of German paintings of the period 1860 to 1930. Return downstairs to see the rooms with an outstanding collection of paintings, sculpture, and china that belonged to the Palatine Electors of the 17th and 18th centuries. After you've seen them, go up one floor to view the paintings and drawings of the Romantic period, the 19th century. The English painter J. M. W. Turner is included among them. Before you leave the museum, visit the delightful tree-shaded garden with its fountain and restaurant.

A little farther along Hauptstrasse, on the left, is the mid-17th-century Providenzkirche (Providence Church), built by Elector Karl-Ludwig just after the Thirty Years' War, the war which pitted Protestants against Catholics in Germany. Continue along Hauptstrasse past Perkeo, the famous old student inn at No. 75, named in honor of the 18th-century court jester who earned immortality through his vast capacity for wine. This inn, founded in 1701, is only one of many throughout the city (most of them clustered along the east end of Hauptstrasse) where students have gathered for centuries. Judging by the crowds which pack the inns for lunch and dinner, they are still favorite meetingplaces, although sometimes tourists seem to outnumber students.

At No. 52 Hauptstrasse is the **Haus zum Riesen** (House of the Giant), named for the statue of its first owner on its façade. This mansion, another example of the architectural skill of Johannes Breunig (who was very busy indeed in Heidelberg), was built in 1707 for Lieutenant-General Eberhard von Veningen. Some of the stone used for this building came from the castle's Dicker

Turm (Thick Tower), blown up by the French in 1689. The mansion now houses university offices. Across the street is the **Friedrichsbau** (Frederick Building), built in 1863 to house the physical sciences. In its front yard is a bronze statue of the chemist Robert Bunsen, professor at the university for forty-seven years, and inventor of the Bunsen burner.

Turn right at the corner to stroll along Brunnengasse (Fountain Lane) and then make a right again at the end of the street along Untere Neckarstrasse (Lower Neckar Street). In the square ahead is the large red sandstone building, the **Stadthalle,** built in the early years of the 20th century as a public hall for concerts and exhibitions. Close by, on the north side of the hall, is the landing from which boats leave for trips on the Neckar River. In warm weather, this is a pleasant way to pass the afternoon. Continue along the south side of the Stadthalle along Untere Neckarstrasse until you come to the huge building called the **Marstall** (Stables). Built in the early part of the 16th century, the Marstall once served as the court stables, an armory, and, today, as a student dining hall.

Turn right along picturesque Schiffgasse (Ship Lane). At No. 4 on the right is a large apricot-colored baroque mansion, Raquet Hettinger House. Notice ahead of you at the end of the street a colorful erker. When you reach Hauptstrasse, turn left and stroll until you come to Heumarkt (Hay Market). Turn left and then right into Untere Strasse. At Pfaffengasse (Priests' Lane), make a short detour to No. 18 on the left, which was the birthplace of Friedrich Ebert in 1871. In 1919, Ebert became the first president of the German Weimar Republic, and served in this position until his death in 1925. Return to Untere Strasse and make the next left into Haspelgasse. On the left at No. 12 is the baroque mansion called Cajeth House. No. 8 is one of Heidelberg's oldest inns, the Schnookeloch, which has been a meeting place for students since 1407, only twenty-one years after the university was founded.

At the end of Haspelgasse, to your right, is another of Heidelberg's famous landmarks, **Alte Brücke** (Old Bridge), with its magnificent classical gateway framed between twin towers with bell-shaped cupolas. The bridge itself is not really that old. It was constructed between 1786 and 1788 by Elector Karl-

Theodor, and is the fifth bridge to cross the Neckar at this point. The four previous ones were destroyed by flood, ice drifts, or fire in the period between 1310 and 1784. The present bridge was blown up in 1945, as were the two other Heidelberg bridges crossing the Neckar, but it was pieced together in 1947. Go beneath the gateway, onto this lovely low-arched bridge, noticing the raised portcullis above. To your left, just beyond the gateway, is a statue of Karl-Theodor with figures of the four great Palatine rivers at his feet: the Rhine, the Danube, the Moselle, and, of course, Heidelberg's own Neckar. At the other end of the bridge is a statue of Pallas Athena with the figures of Piety, Justice, Agriculture, and Commerce at her feet. As you turn around to return to the old city, you have one of the most famous views of Heidelberg—the lovely bridge gateway is directly ahead, the tall tower of the Heiliggeist-Kirche is to the right, and looming over it all is the tremendous mass of the castle, nestled against its green hillside.

Walk through the bridge gateway, then straight ahead along Steingasse (Stone Lane), passing on the right another old student inn, the Goldener Hecht (Golden Pike). Goethe stayed at this inn in 1785 on one of his numerous visits to Heidelberg. Steingasse leads into the narrow Fischmarkt, once the city's fish market. Turn left, walking straight ahead through Marktplatz and along the north side of the Rathaus on Heiliggeiststrasse. This street runs into Hauptstrasse, where, at No. 235, you reach the **Völkerkunde Museum** (Ethnology Museum). Housed in the once-elegant 18th-century Palais Weimar, this museum (hours: Tuesday to Friday, 3–5; Sunday, 11–1) displays changing exhibitions of folk art.

Across the street from the Völkerkunde Museum is the baroque **Buhl House,** distinguished by the handsome steps leading up to its front door. Built in 1710, this mansion was a gift to Heidelberg University in 1907 and is now used for social functions. From the front of Buhl House look to the end of Hauptstrasse to see the neoclassical triumphal arch, the **Karlstor.** It was built in 1781 to commemorate Elector Karl-Theodor.

Return along Hauptstrasse. At No. 217, you pass the Roter Ochsen (Red Ox), probably Heidelberg's most famous student inn. For over 270 years, students have left mementos of themselves—pictures, souvenirs, graffiti—on its walls. Practically next door, at No. 213, is Zum Sepp'l (At Joseph's). Originally built in 1634, the inn was rebuilt after the fire of 1693. Here too generations of students have left souvenirs of their university days. Heidelberg's student inns are unique. To truly savor this old university town, spend some time eating and drinking in its student haunts, most of which have been serving traditionally hearty foods like knockwurst and schnitzel and plenty of good German beer and wine for 250 years or more.

A few steps farther bring you to No. 209, the mansion of Sulpiz and Melchior Boisserée, the two brothers from Maastricht, Belgium. They lived in Heidelberg from 1810 to 1819, collecting paintings of the Romantic period, and their collection later became an important part of Munich's Alte Pinakothek. Goethe stayed in this mansion in the early 19th century as a guest of the Boisserées (he never seems to have gotten very far away from Heidelberg).

Across from the Boisserée mansion is the **Karlsplatz,** occupying the site of a 13th-century Franciscan monastery which was torn down during the Reformation. On the south side of this square is a palatial early-18th-century building which served as the residence of the Grand Dukes of Baden from 1803 until 1918. In 1803, the Palatine territory right of the Rhine river became part of the duchy of Baden. Today the mansion houses the Akademie der Wissenschaften (Academy of Sciences).

Once again stroll along Hauptstrasse, until you reach the **Kornmarkt** (Grain Market), a small square opposite the Rathaus. Dominated by a stone fountain, surmounted by a baroque madonna lifted aloft by angels, this tiny square is lined with picturesque old houses. On the west side of the square once stood the Prinz Karl Hotel, Heidelberg's most elegant hotel in the years 1788 to 1915. It once housed such famous guests as Kaiser Wilhelm I, Prince Otto von Bismarck, the "Iron Chancellor" of the German Empire in the mid-19th century, Kaiser Friedrich III, and Mark Twain. It is now an extension of the Rathaus. No. 5 was once the home of the French emigré Count Charles de Graimberg, who came to visit Heidelberg in 1810 and stayed for fifty-four years. It was Count Graimberg who worked hard to preserve the castle from further ruin during the

19th century, and if it weren't for him, nothing might exist today but a pile of rubble.

Adjoining Count Graimberg's home is the Burgweg (Castle Road), which leads in a few steps to the station, from which you can take the Bergbahn (mountain train), the funicular up the mountainside to Heidelberg Castle. It's only a short trip, but if you prefer to walk, go straight past the hotel and take the stairs on the right, which lead to the main entrance of the castle. Since this excursion will take at least two hours, you might want to save it for another time if you're staying in Heidelberg for a few days. If not, you'll be visiting the castle at the nicest time of the day, late afternoon (if you begin this walk in the morning).

If you take the Bergbahn, get off at the first stop, Station Schloss (Castle Station), and head for the castle. Walk past the small sentry box and over the 18th-century stone bridge, which replaced an earlier wooden drawbridge over the castle's outer moat. Just past the bridge is **Heidelberg Castle,** one of Germany's most magnificent castles. Parts of it date back to the 13th century, when Ludwig I received the castle in fief from Bishop Henry of Worms. The "golden age" of Heidelberg Castle was the 16th and early 17th centuries when a succession of Palatine electors—Ludwig V, Friedrich II, Otto Heinrich, Friedrich IV, and Friedrich V—each altered or added to the castle. Then the castle experienced a series of disasters—fires set by the invading French troops in 1689 and 1693 and another one in 1764, caused by lightning—which reduced much of the once-splendid structure to a gutted ruin. After the 1764 fire, parts of the castle began to be dismantled for use as building materials elsewhere in the town.

To your left is the **Stückgarten** (Battery Garden), built as an additional defense to the west side of the castle by Ludwig V in the years 1528 to 1544. Seventy years later Friedrich V converted the battery into a garden for his English bride, Elisabeth Stuart, daughter of James I. Walk to your left toward the small classical triumphal arch, the **Elisabethenpforte** (Elisabeth's Gateway), built by Friedrich V in 1615 as a birthday surprise (supposedly in one night!) for Elisabeth Stuart. Continue under the arch along the path which skirts the castle's moat. On your right you pass in succession a small 16th-century prison tower called appropriately enough Seltenleer (Seldom Empty), the early-15th-century Ruprechtsbau, the protruding early-16th-century Bibliotheksbau, the early-16th-century Frauenzimmerbau, and, at right angles to this last building, the Englischerbau. The **Englischerbau** (English Building) was built between 1612 and 1615 by Friedrich V, the last of the great princely builders, as a residence for himself and Elisabeth Stuart (hence, its name). Adjacent to this shell of a building is the **Dicker Turm** (Thick Tower), which was once the castle's keep and has twenty-three-foot-thick walls at its base. Its northern half was blown up by the French in 1689. There are two statues on its façade: The one on the left, the tall bearded figure, is of Ludwig V, who erected the Dicker Turm in 1533, and the one on the right is of Friedrich V, who altered the top of this tower in 1619 to make it into a dining hall. Continue past the Dicker Turm to the ruins of a semicircular gun bastion, from which you have a fantastic view over the old town, the mountain across the river, and the Neckar valley beyond.

Return to the Elisabethenpforte, then turn left toward the Brückenhaus (Bridge House), once the gateway guarding the bridge over the moat. Cross the bridge to the Torturm (Gate Tower), the tall square tower with the handsome red sandstone panel above the gateway. This panel, an elegant example of early Renaissance art, once had the Palatinate coat of arms in the center. This has disappeared, but the lions rampant still remain, along with the knights in armor.

Beyond the Torturm you are in the castle courtyard, surrounded by the ruins of magnificent Gothic-Renaissance architecture. During the summer months, this courtyard is the site of plays and concerts, and you can inquire at the tourist office or ask your concierge if anything is scheduled during your stay. Let's begin our survey of these lovely buildings with the **Ruprechtsbau** (Ruprecht's Building), to your immediate left. This simple Gothic structure, dating from about 1400, is the oldest of the residential buildings surrounding this courtyard. The keystone of the arch over the main doorway contains the finest sculpture in the castle—two cherubs rise from the clouds holding a wreath of roses and a compass. There is a legend that the two angels represent the builder's two young sons who were killed in a fall from their father's scaffolding. The wreath of roses is a traditional symbol of death, and the compass represents their father's trade.

Next door is the recessed **Bibliotheksbau** (Library Building), with an elegant oriel on its façade. This Gothic building was erected by Ludwig V in the early 16th century to house his books and artwork. Adjacent to the library is the **Frauenzimmer-bau** (Women's Rooms Building), built by Ludwig V in transitional Gothic-Renaissance style to house the ladies of the court. All that's left today is the magnificent banqueting hall, the Königsaal, which is used for receptions as well as for plays and concerts.

Along the north side of the courtyard is one of the castle's loveliest buildings, the **Friedrichsbau** (Friedrich's Building), added by Friedrich IV in the early years of the 17th century. The façade is an outstanding example of mature German Renaissance architecture. The vertical is emphasized, and the building is crowned with two wonderful two-story gables. The remarkable statues, representing Friedrich IV's ancestors, are all the work of a Swiss sculptor, Sebastian Götz. Some of the statues are: bottom row, far right, Friedrich IV, the Palatine elector who built this structure; second row, far right, Otto Heinrich, who built the structure on the east side of the courtyard; second row, far left, Ruprecht I, the founder of Heidelberg University in 1386; third row, second from the left, Ruprecht III, with his imperial orb and scepter, who became King Ruprecht I of Germany in 1400 and built the Ruprechtsbau; fourth row, far left, Charlemagne, first of the Holy Roman Emperors; and at the top are Spring and Summer with Justice between them.

To the right is a long vaulted passageway leading to a large terrace called the **Altan.** From here, you have another splendid view over the town and river, which is especially impressive at sunset when the entire town seems to glow at your feet. Turn around to examine this part of the Friedrichsbau, which isn't as heavily ornamented as the other side. At the top are the statues of Winter and Autumn, complementing the two statues on the courtyard side of the building. To your left is the 15th-century **Glocken Turm** (Bell Tower), originally an angle defense tower which was later turned into a bell tower and living quarters. It was destroyed by the lightning-fire of 1764.

Return to the courtyard. To your left is the shell of the **Gläserne Saalbau** (Hall of Mirrors Building), with tiers of arcades in the Italian Renaissance style, built by Friedrich II in 1549. The Great Hall on the top floor was lined with Venetian glass mirrors, a novelty and luxury at the time. Along the east side of the courtyard is another lovely Renaissance building, the **Ottheinrichsbau** (Otto Heinrich's Building). This early-Renaissance structure, built in 1556 by Heidelberg's first Protestant elector, Otto Heinrich, predates the Friedrichsbau by half a century. It is decorated with numerous statues, although they are generally inferior to those on the Friedrichsbau. The work of Flemish sculptor Alexander Colin, they represent biblical, allegorical, and mythological subjects: the bottom row, left to right, Joshua, Samson, Hercules, and David; the second row, right to left, Justice with sword and scales, Hope with an anchor, Love with two cherubs, Faith with a Bible, and Strength with a broken pillar—all virtues which a good ruler should possess; third row, left to right, Saturn, Mars, Venus, Mercury, and Diana; and the top row, Sol (the Sun) and Jupiter. These last two rows of statues symbolize the sun, the moon, and the five planets known in the 16th century. Notice the magnificent main doorway in the form of a Roman triumphal arch flanked by four figures. Above the doorway are the Palatine Elector's armorial bearings; in the center is the imperial orb with a cross; on either side is the Palatine lion and the lozenges of the House of Wittelsbach. Above, in a medallion surrounded by cherubs, is a portrait of Otto Heinrich. Beneath the main portal is the entrance to the **Deutsches Apotheken-Museum** (German Pharmaceutical Museum), where you can see utensils and lab equipment from the 17th, 18th, and 19th centuries (hours: 10–5; from December to March, Saturday and Sunday only, 11–5).

Next door to Ottheinrichsbau is the very stark **Ludwigsbau,** built in 1524 by Ludwig V. Finally, rounding out this corner of the courtyard are the kitchens, guardrooms, and the tiny Brunnenhalle (Well Hall), its roof supported by ancient Roman columns from one of Charlemagne's palaces. If you want to, you can take a one-hour guided tour of the inside of the castle (hours: April to September, 9–12, 1–5; October to March, 9–12, 1–4; tickets sold near the Torturm). Even if you decide against a tour, be sure to buy a limited ticket to visit the **Grosses Fass**

(Great Tun) in the cellar beneath the Friedrichsbau. This tremendous vat, built over 225 years ago, and the third one to stand here, holds almost 59,000 gallons of wine when full. The platform on top of it is used for wine tasting or dancing. The wooden statue in front of the vat is Perkeo the dwarf, who was jester to Elector Karl-Philip in the first half of the 18th century. There is a story that Perkeo received his name when he was asked if he could empty the vat at one drink. He answered, in Italian, *"Perchè no?"* ("Why not?"), performed the feat, and got his name. Perkeo has become the symbol of Heidelberg which is appropriate for a city of student taverns. It is said that Perkeo died from drinking a glass of water, his first—and last!

Leave the courtyard, cross the bridge over the moat, and turn left to visit the **castle gardens.** As you stroll alongside the moat you pass the site of the demolished 15th-century **Kraut Turm,** which was blown up by the French. The south face of the tower lies in the moat in one piece just as it fell almost three hundred years ago. Follow the zigzag path along the Great Terrace. These gardens were built in five terraces between 1616 and 1619 by Friedrich V, and they were the marvel of their day, with numerous flower beds, statues, fountains, and grottoes. Friedrich had not completely finished his gardens when he left Heidelberg in 1619 to become King of Bohemia (a title he enjoyed for one winter), an act which precipitated the Thirty Years' War. As you walk along the Great Terrace, you have a good view of the three 15th-century towers to your left: the Kraut Turm, the Apotheker Turm (Apothecary's Tower), the round tower with windows, and the Glocken Turm. Continue to the end of the Great Terrace to **Scheffel Terrace,** named in honor of Heidelberg's most famous poet, Josef Viktor von Scheffel. Once again, you will have a breathtaking view over the city and an interesting view of the castle. You might want to continue strolling through Friedrich's gardens for a while before returning to the old city below.

If you've got a little energy to spare, return to the funicular station and continue up the mountainside. The next stop is **Molkenkur,** 988 feet up, with an interesting view of the castle below. One stop farther brings you to **Königstuhl** (King's Seat), at an altitude of 1,864 feet with a panoramic view of city and valley. Here your walk through Heidelberg ends, high up above the city. If you're lucky, the sun will begin to set, casting a rosy glow on the castle and city below. It's as unforgettable as the Eiskaffee and pastry which you can enjoy on the terrace nearby.

* * *

Find a few hours one morning or afternoon while you're in Heidelberg to take a walk on the Heiligenberg (Holy Mountain) across the river from the old city. You'll be rewarded with magnificent views of the castle as you walk. Begin at the Alte Brücke. Cross the bridge and turn left to stroll along Neuenheimer Landstrasse, which runs parallel to the Neckar. In about three-quarters of a mile you will reach the Bergstrasse. Turn right for a short distance until you come to **Philosophenweg** (Philosopher's Walk) on the right. This is Heidelberg's most famous walk along the slope of the Heiligenberg. As you climb higher, the castle looms closer and larger across the river. If you feel like extending your walk a little, you can return along a path called Oberer Philosophenweg (Upper Philosopher's Walk), which branches off to the left a short distance beyond the lookout point directly opposite the castle. Or you can go still higher to visit the ruins of the 11th-century Benedictine Stephanskirche (St. Stephen's Church) and the Benedictine monastery, Michaels-Basilika, parts of which are 1,100 years old. Not only will you get lots of healthy exercise, but you will enjoy the beauty of this fairy-tale city and its castle from a different perspective.

NUREMBERG

Enclosed within its massive walls, with a castle perched high over the old town and numerous elegant mansions and half-timbered houses, the Nuremberg of five hundred years ago was regarded as one of the most beautiful cities in Germany. It was also one of the most important, standing at the crossroads of several major medieval trade routes. Over the centuries wars intervened and many of the lovely old buildings disappeared. Trade declined with the opening of new trade routes. After each war, the city slowly recovered by rebuilding and expanding, and new and more beautiful buildings appeared. Eventually trade revived, due to the ingenuity and inventiveness of the town's citizens. The worst of the wars—World War II—devastated the city. Yet once again Nuremberg rose from its ashes, to become one of the loveliest and most prosperous cities in Germany. Much survived the great war, and the rest has been restored. Massive walls still encircle the old city. The medieval castle still looms overhead perched on its cliff. Medieval streets lined with gabled mansions and half-timbered houses still wind their way through the old town. It is hard to realize, as you stroll through this charming city today, that so much time and history has passed by, oftentimes catching up Nuremberg in its swift current.

Nuremberg's history began nine hundred years ago, when feudal barons built a castle in the northern part of the old town. A century later, the emperors erected a castle on a cliff high above the town close to the baronial castle. By the middle of the 13th century, Nuremberg had expanded beyond its first set of city walls. It also became an important commercial center because of its strategic location and through the favor of the emperors who sometimes resided here. Nuremberg's golden age was the 15th and 16th centuries. The arts flourished: Hans Sachs was writing his plays and stories, Albrecht Dürer was painting, Veit Stoss was carving, Adam Kraft was sculpting. The 17th century, however, brought the Thirty Years' War and its devastation. Gustavus Adolphus of Sweden occupied the town. Nuremberg went into an economic decline and did not recover for a century and a half.

After the city's annexation to Bavaria in 1806, commerce began to revive. Industry and manufacturing flourished. In the 20th century, Nuremberg became famous—or infamous—as the city where Adolf Hitler's National Socialist Party met annually from 1933 on. During World War II, the city was heavily bombed, and it is miraculous that so much escaped complete destruction. Because of the city's role prior to the war, it was appropriate that the war trials of 1945 and 1946 were held in Nuremberg.

Today, Nuremberg is once again a bustling center of trade in northern Bavaria. It is also once again one of the most beautiful cities in Germany, its old town center studded with numerous fountains, gabled and half-timbered houses, and elegant Gothic churches, survivors of nine centuries of turbulent history. There is so much to see and visit in old Nuremberg that two walking tours, each requiring a full day, are recommended. Plan to spend a night or two in Nuremberg to savor its *Gemütlichkeit*, its numerous beer halls, and the typical Nuremberg sausages called *Bratwürste*.

Begin your first walk through Nuremberg at the **Königstor** (King's Gate), one of the principal entrances to the old city. The Königstor is part of an extensive system of fortifications completed in the mid-15th century consisting of gateways, towers, a double set of walls, and a moat which stretched three miles around the medieval city. These fortifications were the third and final set built to protect the city. The first set was erected in the 11th century, at the same time as the Burggrafenburg (Baron's Castle), and the second in the early 14th century as the town grew. Today the gateways, towers, and walls are almost perfectly intact, but the moat which once encircled the city is now a busy boulevard which follows the old walls and separates medieval Nuremberg from its newer sections.

Walk to your left to visit the **Handwerkerhof** (Craftsman's Courtyard), a lovely section of medieval half-timbered houses, where you can see blacksmiths, potters, and leather workers fashioning beautiful handcrafted items (hours: April to Decem-

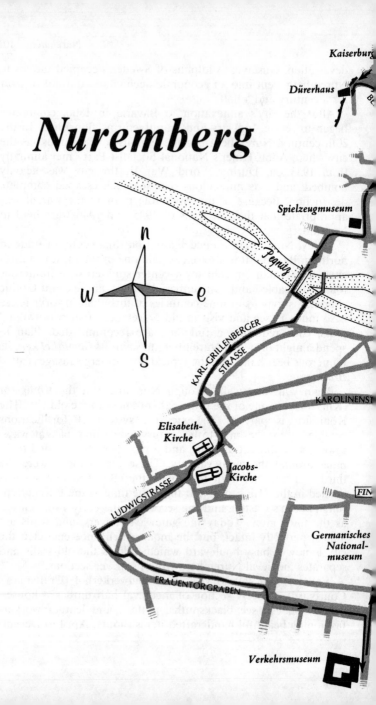

Nuremberg

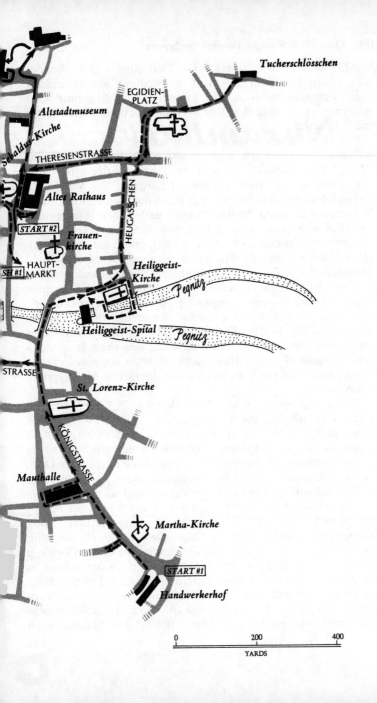

Tucherschlösschen

EGIDIEN-
PLATZ

Altstadtmuseum

Sebaldus-Kirche

THERESIENSTRASSE

Altes Rathaus

HEUGÄSSCHEN

START #2

Frauen-
kirche

HAUPT-
MARKT

SH #1

Heiliggeist-
Kirche

Pegnitz

Heiliggeist-Spital

Pegnitz

STRASSE

St. Lorenz-Kirche

KÖNIGSTRASSE

Mauthalle

Martha-Kirche

START #1

Handwerkerhof

0   200   400
YARDS

ber 23, Monday to Saturday, 10–7; December 1 to 23, Sunday also, 10–7). The combination of the medieval setting and the various artisans busily at work takes you back to a time when machines were unheard of and everything a person needed was made by hand.

Return to Königstrasse (King Street), which begins at the Königstor, and turn left. Königstrasse is the main street cutting through the southern section of the old city. After a few steps you come to the **Martha-Kirche** (Church of St. Martha), a Gothic church erected in the middle of the 14th century. After Nuremberg accepted the Reformation early in the 16th century, the church became a theater. It was here that Hans Sachs, Nuremberg's famous cobbler-playwright, presented many of his plays. Besides making his living at mending shoes, Sachs managed to literally churn out hundreds of songs and stories as well as scores of plays. After his death in 1576, the *Meistersinger* (master singers), comprising cobblers, weavers, tailors, and other men like Hans Sachs, conducted their "singing schools" in the Martha-Kirche until 1620. The *Meistersinger* wrote their own compositions and would sing them in contests before a panel of judges. Hans Sachs and these contests form the subject matter of the popular Wagner opera *Die Meistersinger von Nürnberg*.

Across the street from Martha-Kirche is Luitpoldstrasse, where you will find the Spielwarenhaus Virnich (Virnich Toy Store) at No. 6. Nuremberg has a reputation for being the toy capital of Europe, and you will certainly see numerous toy stores as you stroll around the city today. This is one of the best. Drop in for a few moments to browse among the dolls, trains, and stuffed animals. Return to Königstrasse, and to your left you pass the Gothic Klara-Kirche (Church of St. Clare), once part of an important medieval nunnery. A little further along Königstrasse is the late Gothic **Mauthalle** (Custom House), with its huge steep roof with five rows of dormer windows. The steep gable on the side of the building facing Königstrasse is decorated with an interesting pattern of interlacing niches. Built between 1498 and 1502, the Mauthalle served as a granary before becoming a customhouse in 1572. In 1898 it was converted into an office building. Behind the Mauthalle on

Pfannenschmiedgasse (Tinsmith Lane) is the late-16th-century Zeughaus (Armory).

Once again return to Königstrasse, and turn left. Ahead of you is Nuremberg's largest and most beautiful church, **St. Lorenz-Kirche** (Church of St. Lawrence). The church was begun in 1252 and completed two centuries later. The west façade dating from the middle of the 14th century is most impressive; framed between the two tall towers is the elaborate stone filigree **rose window.** Beneath the rose window is the richly decorated **west doorway,** depicting the major episodes in the story of man's redemption from the birth of Christ to the Last Judgment. Adam and Eve stand on either side of this doorway. Enter St. Lorenz through the south doorway (hours: April to October, Monday to Saturday, 9–5; Sunday, 12–4; November to March, Monday to Saturday, 9–12, 2–4; Sunday, 12–4). As you walk along the nave toward the main altar, notice that the pillars along either side are decorated with statues. Approaching the choir, you pass beneath a magnificent bronze chandelier from the workshop of Peter Vischer, Nuremberg's foremost bronze and brass craftsman. On the pillars just before you enter the choir area are two late-15th-century paintings by Michael Wolgemut, Albrecht Dürer's teacher.

Hanging from the choir vaulting is the unusual wood carving called the **Englische Gruss** (Angelic Greeting). This is the masterwork of Veit Stoss, another of Nuremberg's native sons, and one of the greatest woodcarvers of the Renaissance. Completed in 1518 as a gift to the church of the wealthy patrician, Anton Tucher, the carving shows the Virgin at the moment Gabriel announces that she is to become the mother of God. The two figures are surrounded by a wreath of flowers and six medallions depicting other episodes in Mary's life. Smaller angels flitter about.

Just beyond is the main altar, with a crucifix carved by Veit Stoss in 1500. To the left of the altar is the monumental stone **tabernacle** with scenes from Christ's Passion carved by Adam Kraft between 1493 and 1496. Kraft was another of Nuremberg's native sons and one of the foremost sculptors of his age. This tabernacle is considered his finest work. Beneath the balustrade on which the tabernacle rests is the crouching figure of the sculptor himself, who (with the aid of his two apprentices on either side) symbolically bears the weight of and responsibility for his creation.

Walk behind the main altar along the ambulatory to see the **Krell altarpiece** on the altar in the center. It is interesting since it presents one of the oldest views of Nuremberg. This is the way the city looked five hundred years ago. All of the stained glass in the ambulatory dates from the end of the 15th century and is very lovely. Examine particularly the **Volckamer-fenster** (Volckamer window), two windows to the right of the Krell altarpiece, made in 1487 in the studio of Peter von Andlau. This masterpiece of late Gothic stained glasswork presents the Tree of Jesse, Christ's ancestors traced from Jesse, the Old Testament prophet, to Mary, his Virgin Mother.

To the left of St. Lorenz-Kirche as you stand facing the west doorway is the ornate 16th-century **Tugendbrunnen** (Fountain of Virtue), with bronze statues of the seven cardinal virtues: Wisdom, Prudence, Courage, Faith, Hope, Love, and, on top, Justice with her scales. Notice the marvelous view from here of the Kaiserburg (Imperial Castle) looming over the city in the distance. Across from the fountain is the fortresslike **Nassauer Haus,** an excellent example of a fortified private residence of the Middle Ages. This is the oldest house in Nuremberg, with sections of it dating back to the year 1200. Notice the lovely small 15th-century oriel and the two tiny corner turrets just beneath the roof.

The Karolinenstrasse, which begins in front of St. Lorenz-Kirche, is one of Nuremberg's main shopping streets. Continue along Königstrasse. The next street to the left is Adlerstrasse (Eagle Street), with several interesting old townhouses adorned with oriels and steep gables. This type of building was once very common in Nuremberg and most of Germany. Houses had a limited front facing the street because property taxes were assessed according to the length of the front. The high roof was used to store goods, and the oriels projecting from the façade let in light (a precious commodity in narrow medieval streets, since houses were crowded together) and permitted a view in three directions. These old townhouses were very practically designed to utilize all available space. Make a brief detour along

Adlerstrasse to see Nos. 14 and 16, and particularly No. 21, a mid-18th-century building which is the only survivor of the rococo style in Nuremberg. No. 28 is interesting because it has been modernized, yet still retains two wooden erkers and a corner Madonna.

Just before reaching the bridge, you pass Theinert at No. 2 Königstrasse. This is Nuremberg's largest toy store, and another marvelous place to browse if you are a child at heart. Directly ahead is the Museumbrücke (Museum Bridge), which crosses the Pegnitz River and leads to the northern part of the old city. From the middle of this bridge, you can see the Fleischbrücke to your left, a late-16th-century copy of Venice's famous Rialto bridge. To your right, spanning an arm of the Pegnitz is the picturesque Heiliggeist-Spital (Holy Ghost Hospital), which you will visit in a few minutes. Notice its prominent three-story oriel with the odd-shaped roof.

From the bridge, turn right into Spitalgasse (Hospital Lane), which leads into Hans-Sachs Platz, a square dominated by the monument to Hans Sachs. During his long lifetime (Sachs died at the age of 82), he wrote more than 5,000 songs, 1,600 stories, and 200 plays in addition to making his living as a shoemaker. Today, during the summer months, his plays are presented in the courtyard of the Kaiserburg.

Turn right from the square to cross the Spitalbrücke. On the left is the tall Männerschuldturm (Guilt of Men Tower), built in 1323 as part of the second system of town defenses. Turn right to visit the **Heiliggeist-Spital** (Holy Ghost Hospital), founded by a wealthy Nuremberg businessman, Konrad Gross, as an alms-house for the aged poor in 1339. Part of the hospital sits north of the Pegnitz River, another part is on arches over the river, and part is on this island called Schütt in the middle of the Pegnitz. Go through the outer courtyard and up the stairs to your right into the central courtyard, surrounded by stone arcades topped by wooden galleries. On the northern side of the arcade, see the stone carving of Christ and the two thieves, the work of Adam Kraft (1505). In the adjacent courtyard, near the entrance to the *Weinstube* (a fine place for lunch or dinner, by the way), you see an interesting fountain with a boy blowing a horn, surrounded by a wrought-iron fence.

Return to Hans-Sachs Platz. The façade of the Heiliggeist-Kirche (Church of the Holy Ghost) is to your right. This 14th-century church was where the German imperial jewels were stored for over 350 years before being removed to Vienna in 1796. Today the church serves as a student dormitory. Walk straight through the square into Heugässchen (Little Hay Lane). In a few minutes you will reach Theresienplatz (Square of St. Theresa), with its statue of Martin Behaim, who made the first geographical globe in 1492. Walk to your right through this square into the adjacent Egidienplatz (Square of St. Aegidius). On the right is a statue of Philipp Melanchthon, the German reformer and scholar who was one of the chief followers of Martin Luther. Melanchthon was the author of the Augsburg Confession of 1530, which stated the 17 basic articles of the Lutheran faith. Behind his statue is the Altes Gymnasium, the school he founded in 1526. The building itself dates from 1699. Adjacent to the Gymnasium is the imposing **Egidienkirche,** Nuremberg's sole baroque church, built between 1711 and 1718 on the site of an ancient 12th-century monastery. The interior is stark in its simplicity, with the exception of the choir ceiling. The church also retains several medieval chapels which you can visit, south of the main altar.

On the northern side of the square, behind the equestrian statue of Kaiser Wilhelm I, is the city's archives and library, on the site of the 17th-century Pellerhaus, once one of Nuremberg's loveliest Renaissance residences. The Pellerhaus was almost completely destroyed in World War II, and what remained has been incorporated into the archives. Go into the arcaded courtyard to see the graceful bronze Apollo fountain erected in 1532. Around the base of the fountain cherubs ride sea beasts.

Walk along the north side of the Egidienkirche straight ahead past Webersplatz to Hirschelgasse. To your left is the Renaissance **Tucherschlösschen** (Little Tucher Castle), the home of the Barons von Tucher, built in the mid-16th century. The mansion is furnished with period pieces, and you get an excellent idea of how the aristocrats lived four hundred years ago (guided tours: Monday to Friday, 2, 3, 4; Sunday, 10 and 11; closed Saturday).

Return to Egidienplatz and walk past the church and the Gymnasium into Theresienplatz. Take the first street to the right, Theresienstrasse. In a few minutes, you will pass on the

left Nuremberg's **Altes Rathaus** (Old Town Hall), completed in
1622 by Jacob Wolff the Younger. Walk around the corner to
view the three impressive doorways of this Renaissance structure, and then go into the inner courtyard to see the 16th-
century fountain with a tiny little boy waving the imperial flag
and standing atop a group of dolphins.

Adjacent to the Altes Rathaus is the **Neues Rathaus** (New
Town Hall), completed in 1955. Between the two buildings is the
lovely, small, mid-16th-century **Gänsemännchenbrunnen** (Little
Gooseman's Fountain). A bronze peasant in knickers carries a
goose under each arm, and both geese spurt water from their
beaks.

Return to the front of the Altes Rathaus. Directly before you
is the elaborate, pinnacled east end of the Gothic **St. Sebaldus-
Kirche**. A few feet away to the right on the exterior of the choir
is the sculptured tomb of the Schreyer-Landauer family. This
tomb is rich with reliefs of Christ's Passion and Resurrection,
and was sculptured in 1492 by Adam Kraft. Walk around the
south side of the church to the southwest door to see the
sculptured tympanum depicting the Last Judgment—beneath
Christ's feet the dead climb from their tombs. To the right are
the chained damned, representing all classes of medieval society
being pulled into hell by demons; to the left, angels lead the
saved to Paradise.

Walk around the relatively plain west façade with its two
Romanesque doorways to the north side of the church. For the
moment, walk past the Marienportal (Mary's Doorway) to see
the next doorway called the Brauttür (Bridal Door), which is
adorned with smiling statues of the wise and foolish virgins.
Return to the Marienportal and enter the church (hours: April
and May, weekdays, 9–12, 2–5; June to September, weekdays,
9–6; October, weekdays, 10–12, 2–5; November to March,
weekdays, 10–12, 2–4; November to March, Sunday, 12–4; April
to October, Sunday, 12–5). This beautiful structure, consecrated
in 1273, is a good example of the transition from late Romanesque architecture to early Gothic. As you proceed up the nave,
notice how the style becomes more pronouncedly Gothic as you
approach the late Gothic choir. Opposite the entrance, note the
lovely mid-15th-century altarpiece, the work of an unknown
artist who also painted an altarpiece we will see later in the

Frauenkirche. To the right is a bronze baptismal font, cast about 1430, and believed to be the oldest piece of bronzework in Nuremberg. Behind the font is the St. Peter altarpiece, painted about 1485. Turn around and walk to the right, where the second pillar has a sculptured relief of Christ carrying the cross executed by Adam Kraft in 1506.

Now walk down the center of the nave toward the altar. On the sixth pillar from the west end of the church is an interesting early-15th-century sculpture called the Sunburst Madonna. Continue into the choir to see the church's masterpiece, the **tomb of St. Sebald.** St. Sebald was an 11th-century native of Nuremberg's neighbor, Fürth, and was canonized in 1425. His remains rest in a late-14th-century silver coffin. In 1519, Peter Vischer, Nuremberg's greatest bronze worker, and his two sons completed the fabulous monument which encloses the silver coffin. The bronze work is magnificent, with numerous snails, dolphins, and cherubs. Tiny mice scamper about, and the Apostles stand guard all around. There is a statue of St. Sebald on the west side, and on the opposite end is a magnificent self-portrait of the creator of this monument, a chubby Peter Vischer wearing a leather apron and holding a chisel as if about to add one final detail. This intricate monument is a superior example of German Renaissance bronze casting. Walk behind the high altar to the right to see another masterwork, an extremely realistic **Passion group** sculptured by Veit Stoss in 1520. To the left of this group is the family vault of the Schreyer-Landauers, which you just saw from the outside. Most of the stained glass in the ambulatory is late-14th-century, and is among the oldest in Nuremberg.

Leave the St. Sebaldus-Kirche by one of the doors on the south side of the church and walk toward the Neues Rathaus. Across the street from the New Town Hall you pass Nuremberg's Chamber of Commerce, painted, appropriately enough, with a procession of merchants. Directly ahead is the **Hauptmarkt** (Main Market), where the city's daily fruit and vegetable market is held beneath large colorful umbrellas. This is also the site of the Christkindlsmarkt (Christ Child Market), held annually before Christmas to sell toys and Christmas tree ornaments.

In front of you is the magnificent **Schöner Brunnen** (Beautiful

Fountain), one of the most beautiful medieval fountains in Germany. Completed in 1396 by Heinrich Parler, it is encircled by a late-16th-century wrought-iron grille. There are forty figures arranged in tiers. The bottom row, front, represents philosophy and the seven arts (grammar, rhetoric, dialectics, geometry, arithmetic, astronomy, and music). Seated behind this row are the four Evangelists—Matthew, Mark, Luke, and John—and the four Fathers of the Church—Gregory the Great, Jerome, Ambrose, and Augustine. The middle tier presents the seven electors, who were empowered to elect the emperor, plus three ancient heroes (Hector, Alexander, and Julius Caesar), three Jewish heroes (Joshua, David, and Judas Maccabeus), and three Christian heroes (Clovis, Charlemagne, and Godfrey von Bouillon). This Gothic masterpiece is one of Nuremberg's most well-known attractions.

Another famous sight appears on the **Frauenkirche** (Church of Our Lady), near the Schöner Brunnen: This is the **Männleinlaufen** (March of the Little Men), which occurs every day at noontime. Emperor Karl IV sits enthroned high above the west door, and as the clock strikes twelve, the trumpeters, drummer, flutist, town crier, and bellringer all perform, and out march seven electors to pay homage to the emperor. In order of appearance they are: the King of Bohemia, the Count-Palatine of the Rhine, the Margrave of Brandenburg, the Duke of Saxony, and the archbishops of Trier, Cologne, and Mainz. Three times they parade past Karl IV, who graciously lowers his scepter while up on top a knight and a Turk strike a bell. The Männleinlaufen, installed in 1509, commemorates the Golden Bull issued by Emperor Karl in 1356. This proclamation limited the number of electors eligible to choose a new emperor to seven, and also specified that each newly elected emperor hold his first imperial Diet (Parliament) in Nuremberg.

The Frauenkirche itself, built at the order of the same Karl IV in the middle of the 14th century, is one of the loveliest churches in Bavaria. Go inside a moment through the beautiful west entrance to see the Pergenstorffer monument at the end of the north aisle (hours: April to September, Monday to Saturday, 9–7; Sunday, 12–6; October to March, Monday to Saturday, 9–5; Sunday, 12–5). The charming Madonna was carved by Adam Kraft in 1499. Next to this monument is the mid-15th-century

Tucher altarpiece, painted by an unknown artist for the wealthy Tucher family (whose mansion we visited earlier). In the middle are the Annunciation, Crucifixion, and Resurrection against a gold background. On the wings are St. Augustine and St. Monica (who was Augustine's mother), and Sts. Anthony and Paul. Along the walls of the choir is a host of candle-bearing angels.

Return to the Hauptmarkt to browse among the various stalls. Here, in the midst of some of Nuremberg's loveliest sights, your first stroll ends.

Begin your second walk in the heart of old Nuremberg, the Hauptmarkt. Leave the square at its northwest corner and walk along the street which passes between the Altes Rathaus and St. Sebaldus-Kirche. Past the church the street becomes Burgstrasse (Castle Street) and culminates, appropriately, at Nuremberg's Burg. At No. 15 Burgstrasse is the majestic **Fembo Haus,** the best-preserved example of a Renaissance mansion in Nuremberg. Notice especially the imposing stepped gable with the twin columns, one atop the other. The city once had many such aristocratic residences, but most have disappeared over the centuries, particularly in the bombings of World War II.

The mansion was originally built in the late 16th century as the residence of a wealthy Netherlander fleeing the persecutions of the notorious Duke of Alba who conducted Spanish-style inquisitions in Holland. It later housed a publishing firm and then, about the year 1800, became the property of the Fembo family. Today it is the home of the **Altstadtmuseum,** Nuremberg's city museum (hours: March to October, Tuesday to Friday and Sunday, 10–5; Saturday, 10–9; closed Monday; November to February, Tuesday to Friday, 1–5; Saturday, 10–9; Sunday, 10–5; closed Monday [December 1 to December 23, Monday to Friday and Sunday, 10–5; Saturday, 10–9]). The museum has numerous exhibits on Nuremberg's art and culture from the Middle Ages to the present day. Be sure to visit the top floor where there is a fascinating model of the old city, depicting the way it looked in 1625. There is also a model of the way Egidienplatz, which you visited on your first walking tour, looked before World War II.

Continue up Burgstrasse toward the castle. The castle was once actually two castles: the **Kaiserburg** (Imperial Castle) erected atop the hill in the middle of the 12th century as an imperial residence, and the **Burggrafenburg** (Baron's Castle) built at the foot of the hill in the middle of the 11th century as a residence for the feudal barons who ruled the town. From 1192 until 1420, the Zollerns ruled their Franconian possessions from their castle in Nuremberg and owed their feudal allegiance to whatever emperor happened to be in power. When their castle burned in 1420, they decided to sell the ruin and move out of the town. The castle was never rebuilt, and very little remains of the medieval baronial buildings. Fünfeckiger Turm (Five-Corner Tower), behind and to the left of the building directly in front of you at the end of Burgstrasse, was a watchtower built about the year 1040. It is probably the oldest building in Nuremberg. Also notice the ancient Walpurgis Chapel, which you will pass on your way to the Kaiserburg.

In front of you is the **Kaiserstallung** (Imperial Stables), built in 1495 by Hans Beheim as a granary (hence, the steep roof). It was later used as a stable whenever the emperor visited Nuremberg or an Imperial Diet met in the city. The adjoining building on the right with the tiny corner turrets is the square Luginsland Tower, erected about 1377. Today the Kaiserstallung houses youthful travelers as well as a sound-light-color-and-movement show called the **Noricama** (hours: April to September, end of November to December 23, 10–6; showings each hour). The Noricama serves as an excellent introduction to the city's varied sights, but you may prefer to see it after you've become acquainted with Nuremberg through these two walks.

Now follow the sign saying KAISERBURG toward the castle, passing the baron's Walpurgis Chapel on your right. The Kaiserburg first came into existence in the mid-12th century, and for the next four centuries emperors continued expanding and altering it. The present-day appearance of the castle buildings is largely 16th century. Enter the castle precincts at the **Sinwellturm,** the round watchtower built about 1200 as a lookout point for enemies and fire. The top portion was added in 1561, and you can climb the tower, the highest point in the city, for a panoramic view of Nuremberg. Adjacent to the tower is the Finanzstadel (Counting House), and to its left the lovely half-timbered house used by the bailiff. Both buildings were erected in 1564. To the left in the middle of the courtyard is the 12th-century covered well.

Near the Renaissance gateway, separating the outer and inner courtyards, is the entrance to the **imperial residence,** and there are guided tours if you'd like to see the rooms once occupied by the German emperors (hours: April to September, 9–5; October to March, 10–12, 1–4). Most of this building dates from the 15th and 16th centuries. You will visit the Rittersaal (Knight's Hall), with its heavy oak beam ceiling. Above the Rittersaal is the Kaisersaal (King's Hall), with a ceiling in the imperial colors of black and yellow. The portraits lining the walls are of 16th- and 17th-century Hapsburg emperors. From this room, you pass through a doorway to the emperor's gallery in the chapel. This Romanesque chapel, built about 1200, is actually two chapels, one over the other, joined by an open bay in the center. The upper chapel includes the gallery and was reserved for the emperor, his family, and the closest members of the imperial entourage, while the lower chapel served the remaining members of his retinue.

Return to the outer courtyard to leave the castle. You pass the Heidenturm (Pagan Tower), dating from about 1150 and one of the earliest parts of the Kaiserburg. Next is the Himmelstallung (Heavenly Stable), which sounds as if it housed cherubs and not horses. Now pass through the mid-14th-century Himmelstor (Heavenly Gate), which is appropriately named, as you can look down upon the city below.

Take the stairs to the right and walk along Am Olberg beneath the castle walls. At the end of this street lined with ancient houses, turn left. To your right at No. 64 Obere Schmiedgasse is the late-15th-century half-timbered Pilatushaus (Pilate's House), once the home of plate-armor maker Hans Grünewald. Many craftsmen once lived in this area of the city in the shadow of the Kaiserburg. One of the greatest, Albrecht Dürer, Germany's most famous painter and engraver, lived in the house on the corner diagonally across from Pilatushaus.

Dürerhaus, one of the best-preserved Gothic structures in the city, consists of two sandstone stories and two half-timbered stories topped by a gable roof. The house was built in the middle of the 15th century. Dürer purchased it in 1509 and lived there until his death in 1528. This house makes an interesting contrast to the Tucherschlösschen. The Tucherschlösschen, visited on the first walking tour, was a wealthy aristocrat's home while Dürerhaus was the home of a well-to-do middle-class craftsman. Inside, besides the 16th-century period furnishings, are many of Dürer's original drawings and engravings, as well as copies of the important paintings done while he was living here (hours: March to October, Tuesday to Friday and Sunday, 10–1, 2–5; Saturday, 10–1, 2–9; closed Monday; November to February, Tuesday to Friday, 1–5; Saturday, 10–1, 2–9; Sunday, 10–1, 2–5, closed Monday; if you are here between the end of November and December 23, ask the tourist office or your concierge for the hours the house is open).

As you leave Dürerhaus, notice the section of town wall opposite it. Parts of this wall are mid-15th century, but sections go back to about 1330, when the city stretched beyond its first set of walls. Follow the street directly opposite the gateway, Bergstrasse (Mountain Street), which leads to Albrecht Dürer-Platz, with its statue of the great German painter. Walk straight through the square toward St. Sebaldus-Kirche. On the right is the **Sebald-Pfarrhof** (Parish House of St. Sebald), with its beautiful Gothic oriel. This oriel, a reproduction of the original mid-14th-century one, is one of the most ornate in Nuremberg. Beneath the windows are sculptured incidents from the life of the Virgin.

Walk to the west front of St. Sebald and then straight ahead into the Weinmarkt (Wine Market). Walk to your left into Karlstrasse, where, at No. 13, you come to the **Spielzeugmuseum** (Toy Museum), housed in a Renaissance mansion with an impressive gable. No trip to Nuremberg, Toy Capital of Europe, is complete without a visit to this superior collection of dolls and toys from all over the world (hours: Thursday to Sunday and Tuesday, 10–5; Wednesday, 10–9; closed Monday).

Continue along Karlstrasse to Weintraubgasse (Grapes Lane). Turn right, and soon you are in Maxplatz. Walk past the Albrecht Dürer memorial toward the Maxbrücke. Cross the bridge and walk to your left for a few steps, to enter one of the loveliest corners of old Nuremberg. To your left is the Henkersteg (Hangman's Path), the picturesque covered footbridge over the Pegnitz. The lovely half-timbered building

on the opposite side is the **Weinstadel** (Wine Shed), built about
1448 as a hospital and then converted in the following century
into a wine depot. It now houses students instead of wine casks.
Adjacent to the Weinstadel is the **Wasserturm** (Water Tower),
built in 1325, and once the home of the town's executioner
(hence, Hangman's Path leading to the hangman's home).

The house to the right of the wooden bridge is the Unschlitthaus (Tallow House), built in 1491 as a storehouse for grain. In
1560, the city's tallow offices, whose job it was to tax wax
candles, were established in the Unschlitthaus. In the Unschlitt-
platz is a fountain featuring a bagpiper. Walk past the fountain
and take the street which leads out of the square on the right,
Karl-Grillenberger Strasse. Follow this street as it curves to the
left. At the corner of Karl-Grillenberger Strasse and Ludwigstrasse, turn right. On the right is the neoclassical **Elisabeth-
Kirche,** which once belonged to the Knights of the Teutonic
Order. Its interior is odd; the dome area is disproportionately
high and dominated by too many and too massive pillars. Across
the street is **Jacobs-Kirche,** a Gothic church begun in the early
13th century and not completed until almost three hundred
years later. Go inside to see the unusual blend of Gothic and
modern styles. The 14th-century gilt altarpiece is the highlight of
several interesting medieval art works.

From Jacobs-Kirche, walk directly ahead along Ludwigstrasse
to the **Spittlertor** (Spittler Gateway), part of the 15th-century
town wall. Like several of the city's other 15th-century main
gateways, the Spittlertor was reinforced by huge round stone-
works in the middle of the 16th century.

Leave the old city through this gateway. Turn left to walk
along Frauentorgraben, the site of the great moat which once
encircled the town. After a ten-minute stroll, you will reach
Lessingstrasse on the right. The opera house and theater are on
the left side of the street, and on the right, at No. 6, is the
Verkehrsmuseum (Transport Museum), with exhibits on the
history of railway and postal services (hours: April to September, Monday to Saturday, 10–5; Sunday, 10–1; from October to
March, the museum closes one hour earlier on weekdays). Here,
on the ground floor, you can see the train *Adler (Eagle),* which
ran along the first line opened in Germany (1835). The line was
five miles long, stretching from Nuremberg to Fürth. Passengers

hurtling along at the speed of ten miles per hour could reach Fürth in just thirty minutes.

Return to Frauentorgraben and cross the boulevard. Reenter the old city through the Kartäusertor (Carthusian Gateway) and walk straight ahead to Kornmarkt, once the site of the city's grain market. To your right is the entrance to the **Germanisches Nationalmuseum** (German National Museum), occupying the site of a 14th-century Carthusian monastery. This museum, founded in 1852, contains one of the best collections of art and craftsmanship in Germany, and covers all periods from prehistory to the 20th century (hours: April to September, Tuesday to Sunday, 9–4; Thursday night, also 8–9:30; closed Monday; from October to March, the museum opens at 10).

There are several outstanding items you shouldn't miss seeing as you wander through this huge treasurehouse. On the ground floor is the **Goldkegel von Ezelsdorf** (Gold Cone of Ezelsdorf), a 3,000-year-old cone-shaped helmet of pure gold discovered in a village near Nuremberg. In the room housing objects from the early and high Middle Ages you'll find the **Goldenes Evangelienbuch von Echternach** (Golden Book of the Evangelists), an illuminated manuscript from about the year 1000 with a fantastic golden bejeweled cover. Next visit the former Carthusian church just a few steps away to see Adam Kraft's **Stations of the Cross.** In the small cloister adjacent to the church are several lovely Veit Stoss Madonnas.

Go upstairs to the room housing 16th- and 17th-century crafts to see the **Nuremberg "Egg,"** the first pocket watch, invented by Peter Henlein in 1500. Here also is the first **geographical globe,** completed by Martin Behaim in the same year that Columbus discovered America. Notice that it lacks the Americas. Next door is the fascinating collection of **dollhouses** with period furnishings. Finally, be sure to pay a visit to the room housing **Dürer's work** and that of some of his contemporaries: Lucas Cranach the Elder and Albrecht Altdorfer.

These are just a few of the items you should see. There is much, much more, and you could spend days wandering through these beautifully planned galleries. But it's been a long, busy day of sightseeing, and this is where you end your second walk through Nuremberg.

ROTHENBURG OB DER TAUBER

Rothenburg is, like Heidelberg, a fairy-tale city, the kind of place one pictures while reading a story full of knights performing fantastic feats and damsels in distress languishing in remote towers. The one ingredient Rothenburg lacks, surprisingly enough, is a castle. It once had two, one a ducal palace, the other an imperial residence—but, unfortunately, both disappeared during the Middle Ages. However, the city has all the other necessary prerequisites for a fairy-tale setting, including sturdy medieval defense walls, numerous towers, elaborate gateways, picturesque cobblestone streets, handsome gabled mansions, humble timber-framed houses, and elegant fountains. Rothenburg is one of the best-preserved medieval towns in Germany. To spend a day strolling through its ancient streets and lanes is to get the feel of what it must have been like to live in a medieval town of the 14th and 15th centuries.

Celtic tribes settled in this area nearly two and a half thousand years ago, but Rothenburg's history begins when a castle was built in the area by a 10th-century Franconian duke. Early in the 12th century, Emperor Henry V gave the land around what was to become Rothenburg to his nephew, Conrad of Hohenstaufen. After becoming Emperor Conrad, he decided to build an imperial residence for himself in 1142. The town of Rodenburch quickly grew up around Conrad's castle. The castle was destroyed in an earthquake two centuries later, in 1356; but by that time, the medieval town had expanded to its present size, and was the rival of nearby Nuremberg in population, wealth, and importance.

The 15th century was one of strife and turbulence for the prosperous town. In 1274 Rothenburg had been elevated to the status of a free city by the emperor, but it had to fight to retain this position, due to the jealousy of neighboring towns like Nuremberg and Würzburg. A little more than a century later,

Rothenburg's illustrious *Bürgermeister* (mayor), Heinrich Topp-ler, attempted to include the middle classes in the town govern-ment, and was accused of treason and thrown into prison, where he died in 1408. The guilds continued to agitate for a voice in running town affairs and succeeded briefly in the mid-15th century in taking over the town's governance.

The 16th century was no better. In 1525, the Peasants' Revolt erupted in the Tauber Valley, and hordes of farmers ransacked and looted churches. That same year, Margrave Kasimir of Ansbach quelled the rebellion, occupied the town, and executed the ringleaders in the town's main square. A century later, from 1618 to 1648, Rothenburg found itself in the midst of the Thirty Years' War with Protestants battling Catholics in Germany. In 1631, the troops of Catholic Maximilian of Bavaria under General Tilly conquered the Protestant town and planned to execute Rothenburg's councillors and burn the city. Only the feat of ex-*Bürgermeister* Nusch—the famous *Meistertrunk*—saved councillors and town from destruction (the story of this "master drink" comes up later on during your stroll through the town).

Ravaged by war, plague, and famine, Rothenburg receded into itself from the mid-17th century to the early 19th century. Ironically, it was this poverty which gave us the perfectly preserved town we see today—the town was simply too poor to expand beyond its 14th-century walls or update its medieval dwellings. In 1802, Rothenburg was annexed to Bavaria, and during the 19th century grew into a picturesque tourist center.

Rothenburg's past has not all been fairy-tale prettiness, but what we see and enjoy today as we stroll through this charming medieval town are the remainders of that turbulent era minus the strife and bloodshed. The walls, towers, and gateways which once served to hold off the enemy are now silent and pictur-esque sentinels of a time long gone. The stately mansions, elegant fountains, and cobblestone streets are mute testaments to an age of daring feats and disastrous failures.

Begin your stroll through Rothenburg in the heart of the old town, the **Marktplatz** (Market Square). Dominating the square is Rothenburg's magnificent **Rathaus** (Town Hall), one of the loveliest in Bavaria. The Rathaus is actually two different buildings: The part in front of you is Renaissance, built between

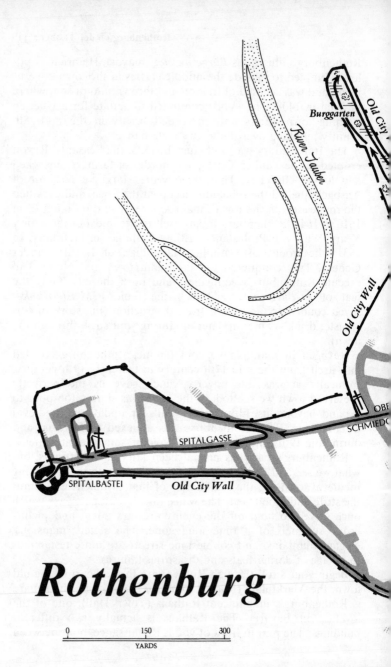

Burggarten

River Tauber

Old City

Old City Wall

OBE

SCHMIEDO

SPITALGASSE

SPITALBASTEI

Old City Wall

Rothenburg

0   150   300

YARDS

1572 and 1578 to replace the building which burned in 1501. This splendid structure, with its octagonal staircase turret, three-story oriel, and imposing south doorway, is the work of Leonhard Weidmann, a native of Rothenburg, whose carved stone head appears at the base of the oriel. The baroque portico was added a century later, in 1681.

Go around the corner past the oriel to see the Gothic portion of the Rathaus, which was built about 1250. Originally the entire building was of this simple, unadorned style. The tall bell tower was added in 1555, and today you can ascend it for one of the best views of this lovely walled city. Four hundred years ago, the town watchman used to scan the surrounding countryside for enemies from this bell tower. Later the tower became a lookout for fire, which, if not checked quickly, could devastate a town in a matter of hours. There is a story told about the watchman who fell asleep while the tower began to burn around him. After this incident, he was required to sound the bell every quarter of an hour to let the town citizens know that he was wide awake.

Return to the baroque portico to enter the Rathaus (hours: 8–6). From a vestibule hung with the coats of arms of *Bürgermeisters* of the past 750 years, you can visit the Gothic Kaisersaal (Imperial Hall), where medieval plays are presented from May to September (hours: summer, 9:30–11:30, 2–4; closed in winter). From the passageway between the Gothic and Renaissance portions of the Rathaus you can also visit the medieval vaults, which display important events in the city's history and facets of its medieval social life. In 1408, in a dungeon beneath these vaults, Heinrich Toppler, Rothenburg's most famous *Bürgermeister,* died mysteriously.

Return to the Marktplatz; to the left of the Rathaus is the 15th-century building with a bell turret called the **Ratsherrntrinkstube** (Town Councillors' Drinking Hall). During the Middle Ages, this drinking hall was reserved for the aristocracy of the town. On the south side of the building is an interesting late-17th-century clock, which presents a famous event in Rothenburg's history seven times a day (at 11 A.M., noon, 1 P.M., 2, 3, 9, and 10). This incident occurred in 1631, during the Thirty Years' War. Protestant Rothenburg sought to repel the Catholic forces of Maximilian of Bavaria with the help of horsemen sent from Würzburg by King Gustavus Adolphus of Sweden. But the assault proved too much: The Rothenburgers were vastly outnumbered by the army under General Tilly, the Swedish horsemen retreated, and the town was forced to capitulate. Tilly was furious at the injuries his forces had sustained and demanded that the town councillors be executed and the town be burned to the ground. Pleading proved futile, until someone had the bright idea of serving General Tilly some of Rothenburg's finest wine, straight from the cellars of the Ratsherrntrinkstube. Of course, Tilly loved the wine, and he started to mellow as he continued drinking. He said he would spare the councillors and the town if someone could empty a six-pint tankard of wine in one long drink without pausing. Ex-*Bürgermeister* Nusch, then seventy years old, volunteered and, as the town citizens watched breathlessly, he gulped down the contents of the tankard without hesitating. Nusch got a tremendous hangover for his efforts, but he saved the town. Seven times a day, now, the windows next to the old clock open and you can see *Bürgermeister* Nusch once again accomplishing his *Meistertrunk* (master drink) while General Tilly looks on, amazed.

Across the square is the lovely **St. Georgsbrunnen** (St. George Fountain), built in the middle of the 15th century and remodeled in Renaissance style in 1608. Atop the pillar is a small statue of George slaying the dragon. Right behind the fountain is the house called the **Fleischhaus** (Meat House). During the Middle Ages, butchers were not allowed to sell meat from their homes, and were fined severely if they tried to do so. So the butchers of Rothenburg banded together and made the Fleischhaus their place of business. Apparently, it wasn't only business that went on here. The upper floor was a dance hall for festivities and special occasions. Today the building is used by local artists for exhibitions (hours: summer only, 9:30–12:30, 2–6). The house with the attractive, turreted oriel adjacent to the Fleischhaus was an apothecary's shop in the late 15th century, and today prescriptions are still filled here.

Past this house **Herrngasse** (Gentlemen's Lane) begins. This is one of Rothenburg's loveliest streets, lined with splendid gabled Gothic and Renaissance patrician mansions. During the Middle Ages, this was the town's most exclusive street, the equivalent of

New York City's Park Avenue, where the wealthiest families lived. On the left side of the street is the Hotel Eisenhut (Iron Hat), considered by many to be the finest small hotel in Germany. It consists of several medieval mansions, some of which are almost eight hundred years old. Across the street is a gaily decorated orange structure built in 1603.

Walk past the curious two-tailed merman fountain to the house at No. 15. It has an interesting courtyard with a half-timbered gallery resting on ancient wooden pillars. Emperor Friedrich III stayed here in 1474. Across the street at No. 18 is another patrician mansion with a fine courtyard, the Von Staudt Haus. Members of the Von Staudt family have been living here for centuries. Directly across the street is Rothenburg's oldest church, **Franziskanerkirche** (Church of the Franciscans), which was once part of a medieval monastery. Built in early Gothic style at the close of the 13th century, the church contains an unusual rood screen separating the choir from the nave (hours: summer, 10–12, 2–4; closed during the winter). Many of the ancient nobility have their tombs and memorials in this church.

Continue to the end of Herrngasse to the **Burgtor** (Castle Gate), Rothenburg's tallest gate tower. Built in the middle of the 14th century, the Burgtor once served as the entrance to the castle of the Hohenstaufens, the imperial ruling family. The castle was destroyed in an earthquake in 1356. Just beyond the gate is the **Burggarten** (Castle Garden), a pleasant public park occupying the site of the former castle. To your left is the small, unpretentious **Blasiuskapelle** (Chapel of St. Blaise), the sole remainder of the Hohenstaufen castle. Built in the early 12th century, the chapel is the oldest existing building in Rothenburg. Past the chapel and the fountain, on the right, is the memorial erected in 1908 to commemorate the five hundredth anniversary of the death of Heinrich Toppler, who governed the town during its golden period, the 14th and early 15th centuries. At that time, Rothenburg was bigger and wealthier than its neighbor, Nuremberg. Toppler died in prison (some say of poisoning) in 1408.

Walk to the end of the garden and up the steps for a fabulous view of the Tauber valley and river. Across the river to your right is an odd miniature castle called the **Topplerschlösschen** (Toppler's Little Castle), built by Heinrich Toppler as his country home in 1388. Turn around for a view of Rothenburg's town walls and towers. These walls, which completely encircle the town, were built in the 14th century, and there are sections along which you can walk (which we will do later on).

Return to the Burgtor, passing between the two quaint 16th-century gate houses, and make the first left turn into Trompetergässchen. Directly ahead is the building called the **Folterkammer** (Torture Chamber), where you can view a grim assortment of medieval torture instruments (hours: summer, 9:30–5:30; winter, 2–4). Turn left on Klostergasse (Cloister Lane) after leaving the Folterkammer. After a few steps you reach the entrance to the **Reichsstadtmuseum** (Imperial City Museum), housed in a mid-13th-century Dominican convent. The convent, established for the daughters and widows of the nobility, was very wealthy in the 14th century. It was taken over by the town in 1544, during the Reformation. Today you can stroll through the convent's early Gothic cloister, kitchen, refectory, dormitory, and apothecary shop, which now house a local history collection (hours: guided tours only, at 10, 11, 2, 3, and 4). There is also period furniture from wealthy patrician mansions, as well as the famous tankard from which Bürger-meister Nusch drank to save the town. Don't miss the interesting collection of paintings by Englishman Arthur Wasse (1854–1930), who adopted Rothenburg as his second home and depicted its lovely buildings and picturesque streets.

Continue strolling along Klostergasse to the huge yellowish-gray sandstone church, **St. Jacobskirche** (Church of St. James), Rothenburg's principal church. Begun in the late 14th century in Gothic style, it is interesting because one of Rothenburg's main streets, the Klingengasse (Lane of Swords), passes right through the west end of the church. Enter St. Jacobskirche through the Brauttür (Bride's Portal), on the south side (hours: summer, 9–6; winter, Monday to Saturday, 10–12, 2–4; Sunday, 11:30–12, 3–4). In the Middle Ages, marriages were blessed in the porch just outside the Brauttür. Even today, engaged couples consider it good luck to enter and leave the church through this doorway. Just to the right of the door is a 15th- to 16th-century carved Agony in the Garden.

Inside, to your left, is the coat of arms of the distinguished

Toppler family, which features two dice, since in the Middle Ages the word *toppeln* meant "to play at dice." Walk down the nave toward the **choir** to see the exquisite stained glass windows and magnificent altarpiece above the high altar with its carved crucified Christ, saints, and angels. On the panels are scenes from the life of the Virgin. Both the windows and altarpiece were the gift of Bürgermeister Toppler, who is buried in this choir. To the left of the high altar is the 15th-century **tabernacle,** with a sculptured Trinity in the middle. In medieval times, this was a place of sanctuary, and if a criminal condemned to death could somehow reach it, he was declared free of guilt and allowed to leave Rothenburg.

Now go to the gallery at the west end of the church to see the church's masterpiece, the **Heilig-Blut Altar** (Altar of the Holy Blood), carved by one of the greatest German Renaissance sculptors, Tilman Riemenschneider of Würzburg. Completed in 1504, this magnificent piece of woodcarving consists of three panels. On the left is Christ entering Jerusalem in triumph, and on the right is the Agony in the Garden. The middle panel presents the Last Supper at the moment when Christ reveals that one of his own Apostles is planning to betray him. Notice the taut, perplexed expressions on the faces. The entire scene, with the exception of Judas, who stands facing Christ, was carved from one piece of limewood. Above the altarpiece is a Romanesque cross containing a relic of the Holy Blood.

Leave St. Jacobskirche through the Brauttür, turn left, and walk around the east end of the church into Kirchplatz (Church Square). The building directly ahead with a staircase turret capped by a bulbous dome is the **Gymnasium.** It was built in Renaissance style at the end of the 16th century by Leonhard Weidmann, the architect of the Renaissance portion of the Rathaus, as a school for boys.

Cross the Kirchplatz into the adjacent Marktplatz. Walk diagonally across into **Obere Schmiedgasse** (Upper Smith Lane), another of Rothenburg's lovely medieval streets lined with the homes of the nobility and wealthy craftsmen of 500 years ago. There are also many interesting guild signs you will spot as you stroll along, such as two lions with a pretzel in the middle, which denotes a baker, and a round copper plate that designates a barber (in the Middle Ages, barbers also functioned as assistants to surgeons, and in cases of bloodletting—a medieval cure-all—they were required to hold a copper plate for the surgeon). There are also other more easily recognizable signs.

At No. 3 on the left side of the street is one of Rothenburg's most attractive houses, the elaborate **Baumeisterhaus** (Master Builder's House). Leonhard Weidmann, architect of the new Rathaus and the Gymnasium, built the house for himself in 1596. The bottom floor served as a combination stable-garage for horses and carriages. The next two floors were the living quarters, and Weidmann decorated these two levels with fourteen stone figures, the seven cardinal virtues on the first floor and the seven deadly sins on the second. The top three floors were granaries or storehouses, and on either side of these stories you see stone dragons. This type of house, a common sight throughout Germany and the Netherlands in the 16th century, maximized efficient use of space. The Baumeisterhaus is now a restaurant; you can eat in the interior courtyard in summertime, surrounded by wooden galleries.

Next door, at No. 5, is the Gasthof zum Greifen (Inn of the Griffin), once the home of *Bürgermeister* Heinrich Toppler. Continue down the street to No. 21, the Roter Hahn (Red Cock), which was the home of *Bürgermeister* Nusch in the 17th century. Across the street from Mayor Nusch's home is the unusual Gothic **St. Johanniskirche** (Church of St. John). The bottom half of this church served as a place of worship, while the top portion was a granary.

Past the church, Obere Schmiedgasse becomes Untere Schmiedgasse (Lower Smith Lane). Stroll ahead to the **Plönlein** (Little Place), a picturesque corner with half-timbered houses and a fountain. The street divides here; take the one which descends to the mid-14th-century Koboldzellertor (Koboldzeller Gate). Go through this ancient gateway and descend the hill, passing the Kohlturm (Coal Tower) to your left. Just past the arch you have a spectacular view of the countryside beyond Rothenburg's walls.

Return now to the Plönlein and walk toward the Siebersturm, another of Rothenburg's 14th-century towers. This one is distinguished by its clock. Walk under the tower into Spitalgasse

(Hospital Lane). Just past the tower, look back to see a stone face high up between two small windows. During medieval times it was believed that this face could avert the plague from the town. Stroll along Spitalgasse until you come to Rossmühlgasse (Horse Mill Lane) on your right, which leads to the tall building called the **Rossmühle,** erected in 1516 to mill and store flour. The mills were turned by horses (hence, the name).

Return to Spitalgasse; in a few steps you pass the **Spitalkirche** (Hospital Church) with its slender tower. This church was begun in 1308 and did not reach completion until the early 16th century. Next door to the Spitalkirche is the **Spital,** a huge Renaissance building erected in 1575 by the town's busy architect, Leonhard Weidmann. Today it is a home for the elderly. Walk beneath the arch to the left of the Spital, which leads you to the lovely small **Hegereiterhäuschen** (Gamekeeper's Cottage), with its elegant staircase turret and unusual high-pointed roof. This little house was built in 1591 as the lodging for the hospital's superintendent of estates. Straight ahead is the Zehntscheune, a long building used as a granary, and to its right is the Stöberleinsturm, with four little oriels at its corners along the top.

Return to Spitalgasse once again, continuing toward the tall tower forming part of the **Spitalbastei** (Hospital Bastion). This was built in the 16th and early 17th centuries, much later than most of the town's towers and walls. It is an interesting fortification, consisting of two oval courtyards. Go through both courtyards for a view of the defenses from the outside. Return by turning right and crossing over a quaint old wooden bridge. This will bring you to the stairs leading to the covered arcade along the town's 14th-century **ramparts.** At the top of the steps turn left and stroll beneath the arcade, from which you have interesting views of the town below. You will pass in succession the Kleiner Stern (Small Star Tower), Grosser Stern (Big Star Tower), Faulturm (Rotten Tower), Schwefelturm (Sulphur Tower), and Hohennersturm (Hohenner Tower) before coming to the **Rödertor** (Röder Gateway), the elaborate west gateway into Rothenburg. Descend the steps here to view this picturesque early-17th-century bastion, which consists of an archway, two small gatehouses, an inner archway, and a tower with four oriels just beneath its roof.

Stroll up Rödergasse toward the Markusturm (St. Mark's Tower) and the adjacent **Röderbogen** (Röder Arch). Past the fountain, you reach this interesting archway with its clock, tiny steeple, and tower, which were once part of Rothenburg's earliest city wall, constructed in the 12th century. Between the 12th century and the 14th, the town expanded greatly and the second line of towers and defense walls you just walked along was built. Some of the more elaborate bastions, such as Spitalbastei and the Rödertor, were added on a couple of centuries later.

Go under the arch. Adjacent on the right is the medieval Buttelhaus, where the town jailer once lived. Turn right to walk along Milchmarkt (Milk Market). Past the fountain, you see to your right the lovely **Weisser Turm** (White Tower), another part of the old 12th-century town wall. Go beneath the tower, and adjacent to the Weisser Turm on the left is the picturesque 16th-century **Judentanzhaus** (Jewish Dance House). Notice the half-timbering on its upper stories and the lovely oriel projecting into the street. The Galgengasse (Gallows Lane) which starts at this tower led to the medieval place of execution.

Turn around, walk beneath the Weisser Turm again, and make a right into Sulzengässchen (picturesquely named Little Pickled Meats Lane). At the end of this small street, turn right for a few steps, and make the first left turn into Judengasse (Jews' Lane), site of the former ghetto. Jews were not permitted to have gables on their houses, so you can tell at a glance which homes were once inhabited by Jews. This street leads to Klingengasse (Lane of Swords). Make a short one-block detour to the left to see the **Feuerleinserker,** a very beautiful early-17th-century oriel which was part of an equally lovely stone and half-timbered house.

Return along Klingengasse toward the **Klingenturm,** another picturesque tower, complete with a set of oriels and tiny bell lantern atop its roof. This tower and its archway is the main north entrance to the town. Go beneath the arch, and directly ahead is **St. Wolfgangskirche** (Church of St. Wolfgang), an interesting late Gothic church dating from the end of the 15th century. The church is connected to the Klingenturm by a curved 16th-century stone bastion, thus making the church part of the town's defenses. Step inside a moment to see its simple interior (hours: summer, 10–12, 2–6; closed in winter). Notice that there are windows only on the south side; the north side was the town wall.

From here return via Klingengasse, Kirchgasse, and Herrngasse to the Marktplatz, where you may be in time to see one of the performances of the old clock. Your walk through this charming medieval German town is now over. And the Ratsherrntrinkstube nearby is a perfect spot to reward yourself with a stein of beer or a glass of wine.

HOLLAND

DELFT

Picture a typical Dutch postcard which you can buy in any one of a dozen towns in Holland: There are lovely Renaissance mansions reflected in a peaceful canal, a tiny stone bridge in the corner crossing the canal, and perhaps a tall church steeple looming over everything in the background. This is Delft, which is bóth the classical Dutch town, with its mansions, canals, and churches, and, at the same time, the more-than-typical town: Delft is lovelier. Its canals are more placid, its mansions more elegant, and its church steeples more predominant than in the typical Dutch town. Its postcard loveliness is more than mere surface beauty—Delft is a real town full of life and vitality. The market square bristles with activity, the canals carry water traffic through the heart of the old town, and the people are friendly and lively.

Delft is a comparatively new European city. In 1246, after being given its first city charter, Delft quickly grew into a weaving and woolen center. In 1536, fire destroyed much of the town, and again, in 1654 a monumental gunpowder explosion destroyed a huge part of it. But despite both disasters, Delft continued to grow in commercial and, even more important, in political power. In the mid-16th century, Prince William of Orange, called William the Silent, made Delft his headquarters in his organized resistance against Spanish domination of the Low Countries. The Union of Utrecht, uniting the seven northern provinces against the Spaniards, was signed in 1579. Five years later, William was assassinated by an agent of the Spanish king, Philip II. His efforts, however, eventually led to independence and to what would later become The Netherlands.

The 17th century, Holland's "golden age," was a time of progress for Delft as well: The arts flourished, elegant mansions were built along Delft's canals, the ceramics industry thrived, and Delft blue china became famous the world over. At the end of the 17th century, the French revoked the Edict of Nantes,

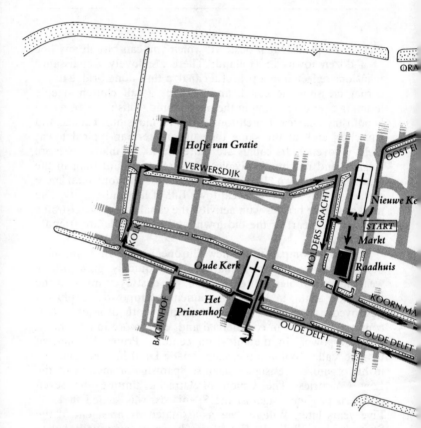

Hofje van Gratie

VERWERSDIJK

OOST EI

Nieuwe Ke

START

Markt

VOLDERS GRACHT

Oude Kerk

Raadhuis

KO

KOORN MA

BAGHINHOF

Het
Prinsenhof

OUDE DELFT

OUDE DELFT

Delft

0   250
   YARDS

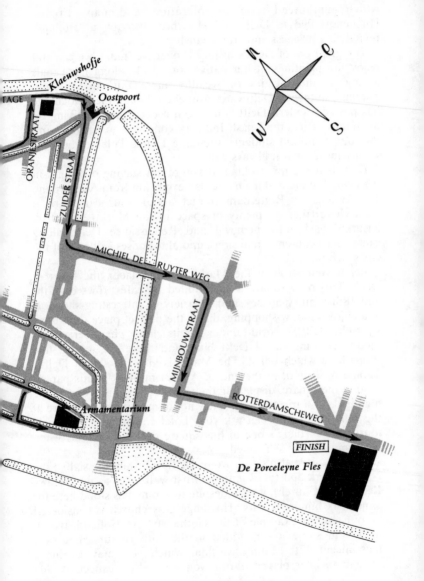

which guaranteed religious toleration, and many French Huguenots fled to Delft and elsewhere throughout Holland, revitalizing business and craftsmanship.

The great era of Delft's history is over, yet today we can still enjoy the paintings of her native sons, walk along her canals gazing at the façades of wealthy merchants' homes, and purchase authentic Delftware. And even though the golden age has passed, modern Delft is far from a decaying city living on memories of its grand past. Industry continues to flourish, and the nine thousand students attending Delft's Polytechnic University insure that it always will.

Delft is made for strolling. If you're not staying overnight in the town, but are making a one-day excursion from Amsterdam, The Hague, or Rotterdam, forget about your car. Park it somewhere (there is plenty of space in the Markt) and stroll leisurely back into medieval and Renaissance Delft, along canals, past churches, mansions, and almshouses—all part of the city's rich past.

Begin your stroll in the **Markt** (Marketplace), the heart of Delft. This busy square is surrounded by cafés, rows of 17th- and 18th-century houses, and a variety of interesting shops. If you enjoy window-shopping, this is the perfect place to indulge yourself. Delft is world-famous for its china, characterized by unique coloring called Delft blue, and there are several fine shops here which sell it. The Markt is also the site of Delft's Taptoe or Tattoo; at the end of August military bands parade around the square, displaying their virtuosity. This is one of the highlights of a trip to Delft, so try not to miss it if you're here at the right time. You can ask your hotel concierge or the local tourist office (there's one in this square near the church) when performances are scheduled.

In this square also stand two of Delft's outstanding sights: the Nieuwe Kerk and the Raadhuis. First walk over to the **Nieuwe Kerk** (New Church), which, despite its name, has stood here for almost six hundred years. This huge gray church is considered an outstanding example of the Gothic style in Holland. Its tall brick and stone tower, added in the 15th century, houses a magnificent 17th-century carillon, which you may be lucky enough to hear played during your visit. You can climb 365 steps to reach the top of this tower (hours: May to mid-September, daily, 10–4:30). On a clear day you will have a marvelous view of Delft's patchwork of canals, bridges, and Renaissance houses.

Walk into the church (hours: April to October, weekdays, 9–5; November to March, weekdays, 10–12, 1:30–4). The stone pillars on either side of the nave support a brick upper portion, and along both outer walls of the choir are colorful stained glass windows, which were completed in 1936. But the highlight of this church is the magnificent baroque **sarcophagus of William the Silent,** one of the heros of Dutch history. As Prince William of Orange, he organized the Dutch nobility into rebellion against the harsh, absolutist rule imposed on Holland by Spain's King Philip II (Holland was, in the 16th century, part of the huge Spanish empire). In 1567, Philip sent his general, Fernando Alvarez de Toledo, the third Duke of Alba, to the Low Countries as his governor. Alba's cruelty further alienated and united the Dutch in resistance to Spanish rule. For a time, William was forced to retreat to Germany, where he continued his efforts with the aid of Dutch privateers. In 1584 he was declared Count of Holland.

William's white marble effigy lies atop a black marble sarcophagus surrounded by twenty-two slender marble columns. At his feet rests his faithful dog, who supposedly saved his master from an assassination attempt in 1572. The corners of the canopy over the sarcophagus are supported by the allegorical figures of Justice, Liberty, Religion, and Valor, and at the head of the tomb sits another effigy of William, this one in full armor. The elaborate tomb is the work of Hendrik de Keyser and his son, Pieter, and was completed in 1621, 37 years after William's death. Beneath the sarcophagus rest the remains of William and some forty princes and princesses of the House of Orange-Nassau.

Behind William's sarcophagus, to the right, is the monument to King William I, who died in 1843. Above it is a tablet with a relief by the Italian sculptor Canova, in memory of Prince William George Frederick of Orange, who died in 1799. On the north side of the choir is the **monument of Huig de Groot,** known as Grotius, with an epitaph describing him as "the wonder of Europe." Grotius, who died in 1645, is best known as the "father" of international law. In 1625, he published his *De Jure Belli ac Pacis,* still used by law students today, which defined the doctrine of natural law as relating not only to individuals but also to states. This church has a splendid organ, and recitals are frequently given in the summertime. Before leaving the church and returning to the square, you might ask when the next recital is scheduled.

As you leave the Nieuwe Kerk, notice the statue of Grotius to the right. Now cross the square to Delft's **Raadhuis** (Town Hall), with its cheerful red shutters and ornate baroque ornamentation. The Raadhuis was built in 1618 by Hendrik de Keyser. The belfry, however, is 14th century and belongs to the earlier Town Hall, which was destroyed by fire in 1536. Inside (hours: Monday to Friday, 9–5) are several outstanding paintings by the 17th-century Delft artist Michiel van Miereveld. On the upper floor, in the Trouwzaal (Marriage Hall), see his corporation piece, *Banquet of the Arquebusiers* (soldiers who carried a firearm called the harquebus), painted in 1611. Corporation pieces were group portraits of individuals belonging to a common organization, such as soldiers or directors of an almshouse or orphanage. They were extremely popular in 17th-century Holland, and many of the great artists of the day, including Rembrandt and Frans Hals, painted them. On the same floor is the Council Chamber, with portraits of various princes of Orange-Nassau. Interspersed around the building are paintings of the city of Delft as it looked 350 years ago. It seems to have changed very little in all that time.

Leave the Raadhuis and go around the building to the right. Directly in front of you is the ancient Boterhuis (Butter House), once the site of the Butter Market. To its right is a building called the Waag, with its frieze of a scale, barrels, and sacks. Goods were officially weighed here. At one time the Waag also housed the guildhall of the goldsmiths and silversmiths. Walk to the right of the Waag and over the tiny bridge, across what was once Delft's wine harbor, Wijn Haven. Turn left, and after a few steps you will be walking along **Koorn Markt** (Corn Market), one of Delft's many lovely canals, lined with picturesque houses and crossed by high arching bridges which allow the water traffic to flow beneath. One of the loveliest ways to tour Delft—after you've completed your walking tour of the city—is by boat. It's interesting to see all the buildings you've visited from a different perspective. At the corner of Koorn Markt and Peperstraat there are boats which will take you on a one-hour water tour of the city (hours: April to September, every hour from 10 to 5).

While walking along Koorn Markt, notice some of the lovely patrician mansions, particularly No. 81. Continue on until you come to No. 67, the **Paul Tetar van Elven Museum,** which occupies a mansion. Paul Tetar was a teacher and a minor 19th-century artist. When he died in 1896, he left a will stipulating that his home become a museum and that no admission fee ever be charged. As you walk through Tetar's home, you travel back to see how a wealthy individual lived in the Delft of the early 19th century. The house is furnished in the style of the period and has a good collection of porcelain and paintings. There is even an atelier—Tetar must have painted in comfort in his lovely home. Continue along Koorn Markt. Across the canal from the splendid house at No. 41 is a former synagogue, now used by the university's music faculty.

At the end of Koorn Markt on the right you see the 17th-century **Armamentarium,** once the city's military arsenal. Turn around and return to the intersection of Koorn Markt and Bree Straat. Make a left, and shortly you come to **Oude Delft** (Old Delft), the city's oldest waterway, which has been in use for almost one thousand years. Oude Delft is also one of Delft's loveliest canals. It stretches from one end of the inner city to the other, and is lined with numerous 17th- and 18th-century houses and crossed by tiny arched stone bridges. Oude Delft looks as if it came straight out of a storybook, but it's better than fantasy, since you can actually stroll along enjoying the reflections of the quaint houses in the water and watching the boats and ducks slowly drift by.

Before strolling back toward the center of the city, however, turn left to see No. 39. This 17th-century building with stepped gables was once the home of the **Dutch East India Company,** which built the vast Dutch commercial empire in the Far East. This area of the world still influences the Dutch; witness the numerous Indonesian restaurants throughout Holland (particularly in the large cities) where you can sample a rijsttafel (rice table), a feast consisting of rice plus at least a dozen accompanying small dishes. The Dutch East India Company building now houses one division of Delft's Polytechnic University, the architectural school.

Retrace your steps and proceed along Oude Delft. No. 137 was once an orphanage for boys, and the one directly across the canal was for girls. Next door to the girls' orphanage is the late-14th-century Roman Catholic chapel of St. Hippolytus. You pass the Renaissance house at No. 157, once occupied by Pieter de Hooch. Hooch, a native of Rotterdam, was a contemporary of Delft's native son Jan Vermeer. Both painters were intrigued by the effects of sunlight on house interiors. A few steps farther on is the **Gemeenlandshuis** (Inland Polders Authority), No. 167. This mansion, with its elaborate Gothic façade rich in red, blue, and gold coats of arms, has the distinction of being the oldest private dwelling in the city—it is over 450 years old. It has the further distinction of having served as the headquarters of the last two titular rulers of Holland, the Spaniards Charles V and Philip II, when they visited Delft in the 16th century.

Cross the next bridge to the **Oude Kerk** (Old Church) and walk along Heilige Geestkerkhof (Holy Ghost Churchyard) to reach the main entrance to the church. If you're passing this way on a Thursday, you will find the flower market in full swing on nearby Hippolytusbuurt to the right of the church entrance; stop to browse among the innumerable varieties and colors of Dutch flowers. This large red brick church is at least a century older than the Nieuwe Kerk. It was begun in the 13th century, but did not reach completion until the 15th century. Its bell tower—the leaning tower of Delft—is almost seven hundred years old and houses an ancient bell which is rung only on momentous occasions, because of its tremendous weight (it is the heaviest bell in the Netherlands). Go inside (hours: April to September, weekdays, 9–5; October to March, apply for admission at No. 1 Heilige Geestkerkhof) to see the brilliant **stained glass windows,** the work of Joep Nicolas, who completed them in 1972, and the carved mid-16th-century pulpit. But the principal reason for visiting the Oude Kerk is to see the tombs of three famous Dutchmen. At the west end of the north aisle is the **wall tomb of Antonie van Leeuwenhoek,** the inventor of the microscope, who died in 1723 at the age of ninety-one. Here also rest the bodies of two famous 17th-century Dutch admirals, **Piet Hein** and **Maarten Tromp.** Hein, who died in 1629, commanded Holland's fleet in the revolt against Spain and became commander-in-chief of the entire Dutch navy the year before he died. His monument in the choir is the work of Pieter de Keyser. Tromp, who was killed in a sea battle in 1653, was successful in defeating the combined fleets of Spain and Portugal in 1639. Thirteen years later, he made Holland mistress of the seas for a brief time by defeating the English fleet under the command of Admiral Robert Blake. There is a legend which grew up after Tromp's defeat of Blake: He is said to have hoisted a broom up his masthead to indicate that he had succeeded in sweeping the seas clean of the British. His victory was short-lived: Tromp was killed the following year. Tromp's monument in the chapel, to the left of the choir, depicts his last sea fight, and is the work of Rombout Verhulst and Willem de Keyser. This church also presents organ recitals, so don't forget to inquire about when the next one is scheduled.

Return along Heilige Geestkerkhof, cross the bridge and walk almost straight ahead into St. Agathaplein to visit Delft's **Ethnological Museum,** at No. 4 (hours: weekdays, 10–5; Sunday, 1–5). Here you can view an interesting collection of artifacts from Indonesia. Directly opposite is **Het Prinsenhof** (Princes' Court). This building was once the convent of St. Agatha, founded about the year 1400, and it became one of the wealthiest and most powerful in Holland during the later Middle Ages. After the Reformation the convent was dissolved, and became the home of William the Silent. Later the building was used as a warehouse, and today it holds several interesting "museums within a museum" (hours: weekdays, 10–5; Sunday, 1–5).

From the ticket booth, walk straight ahead. In the first large room you come to, you pass a curious half-carved, half-painted triptych. The next room, the former convent's refectory, has an interesting painted ceiling and numerous portraits. At the end of this room, on the left, is the circular staircase at the foot of which William the Silent was murdered by Balthazar Gerards at the instigation of the Spanish King Philip II on July 10, 1584. You can still see the bullet holes in the wall. At the top of the stairs to the right are rooms hung with portraits of former Stadholders (Princes) of Holland with their consorts. Included among these are William the Silent and his consort, Mary, who both crossed to England in 1688 to become joint rulers after Mary's father, James II, was deposed. Just beyond these rooms is the 15th-century **chapel,** with wooden statues beneath the vaulting ribs, and more portraits. Other rooms in the Prinsenhof contain tapestries, paintings, and china. There are also rooms displaying curious mementos which belonged to the royal family and their predecessors, the Stadholders. Another part of the museum is devoted to the Eighty Years' War of 1568–1648, the War of Liberation, which pitted Spain against Holland.

Return to Oude Delft and turn left. At No. 183b you pass Het Scheppend Ambacht (Creative Craft), where you can see and buy from a collection of contemporary handicrafts (hours: Tuesday to Saturday, 9–12:30, 1:30–5:30). At No. 199 is the **Huis Lambert van Meerten Museum** (hours: weekdays, 10–5; Sunday, 1–5). This extraordinarily lovely mansion houses one of the best collections of old Dutch tiles in Holland, but there are also tiles from other European countries. The mansion also contains magnificent silver collections and furniture of the 16th to 18th centuries. As you walk from room to room, notice the beautiful woodwork, particularly the hand-carved doors, but especially notice the splendid rooms and their furnishings.

From the museum turn left, and after a few yards, near a small bridge, you come to the former Bagijnhof, with its weather-worn doorway. At one time the Bagijnhof was the home of a community of lay nuns, called the Beguines or the Sisters of the Blessed Sacrament. Originally founded in the 7th century by St. Begga, this community was unusual in that the sisters did not take religious vows or live together communally. Each one had her own little house. They did, however, come together for prayer, and each nun was bound by certain rules. Today you can still see Bagijnhofs in Holland and Belgium. Here in Delft is one example of the community's central courtyard surrounded by tiny houses. To visit the chapel, ring the bell at either No. 23 or No. 25.

Cross the bridge in front of the Bagijnhof and continue walking along Oude Delft to the street called Kolk (Pool). Turn right where Kolk leads into Molenstraat (Mill Street). At the end of this street, cross the bridge and turn right into Verwersdijk. At No. 154, walk down the alleyway to see the **Hofje van Pauw** (Peacock Almshouse), which has served as a refuge for poor, elderly married couples since 1707. Its courtyard is an oasis of peacefulness. Walk through the garden and under the arch. Turn right and then right again at the corner. The **Hofje van Gratie** (Grace Almshouse) will be on your right. This almshouse has been serving poor unmarried women for the past four hundred years. If you would like a peek at its Regents' Room, apply for admission at No. 24 (hours: Wednesday and Saturday only, 1–5).

Return to Verwersdijk, turn left, and stroll along, enjoying the ancient houses and the canals. Verwersdijk becomes Vrouwjuttenland, and leads to the intersection of Vrouwenregt (Womens' Rights) and Vlamingstraat, from which you have a picture-postcard view of the Nieuwe Kerk. Turn right, cross the bridge, and walk along **Volders Gracht** (Fullers' Quay), named in honor of the men whose job it was to clean and thicken wool before it was dyed. This is one of Delft's loveliest canals: The houses on the opposite side rise sheer from the water, and over it all looms the tower of the Nieuwe Kerk. At the end of Volders Gracht, on the right, is a building with ornamental cow heads—appropriately enough, it was once Delft's Butchers' Guildhall.

Return through the Markt to the south side of the Nieuwe Kerk and walk along Oude Langendijk. Cross the bridge and turn right along Oost Einde (East End) until you come to Oranjestraat on your left. At the end of Oranjestraat, turn right along Oranje Plantage (Orange Estate), one of the boundaries of the inner city. At No. 58 is the **Klaeuwshofje,** a Roman Catholic almshouse, which has been functioning since 1605. Step inside to see the tiny houses neatly arranged around a pretty little garden.

A little farther on is the **Oostpoort** (East Gate), a picturesque 14th-century town gate, and the sole survivor of the seven gates which once surrounded the inner city. The others were completely destroyed in the great fire of 1536, which razed so much of Delft.

Finally, to complete your tour, visit the Royal Delftware

Chinaworks, called **De Porceleyne Fles** (China Vase). Since it's a mile's walk from the Oostpoort, you might want to find a taxi, but if you're up to adding another mile to your feet, the factory is not too difficult to reach. From Oostpoort walk south along Zuider Straat until you come to Michiel de Ruyter Weg. Turn left, stroll to Mijnbouwplein (Mining Square), and make a right along Mijnbouw Straat to reach Rotterdamscheweg. Turn left, and at No. 196 you come to De Porceleyne Fles (hours: April to mid-October, weekdays, 8:30–5:30; Sunday, 1–5:30; mid-October to March, weekdays, 9–5).

The china industry began in Delft during the 16th century, when Dutch adventurers returned home with Oriental porcelain, which the enterprising Dutch began to imitate. By the mid-17th century, china manufacturing was flourishing in Delft and elsewhere and there were 30 factories in Delft alone producing fine ceramics. All of them disappeared 150 years later during the French Revolution. De Porceleyne Fles, originally founded in 1653, was re-founded in 1876 and, today, if you are here between April and the middle of October, you can watch Delft porcelain being made the same way it was three hundred years ago. The lovely blue color which is characteristic of Delft china comes only after glazing. The clay is molded and fired; paint is applied in a design, but the color at this point is black. A glaze is then applied, and the china is fired once again. The black design now turns blue—Delft blue. Here at De Porceleyne Fles, amid the exquisite products of Delft's craftsmen, your stroll through this lovely Dutch city ends.

UTRECHT

Although Utrecht is the fourth largest city in Holland and a bustling center of trade, it gives the impression of being a much smaller place than it actually is. This is mainly because many parts of the city, like those we will see and visit during our walks, convey the essence of small-town Dutch life. There are the tree-lined canals, unique for their double-decker sidewalks, patrician mansions sandwiched in among much more modest dwellings, numerous Romanesque and Gothic churches, medieval alms-houses, orphanages, and hospitals which dot the city. You'll find these sights all over Holland, but here in Utrecht not only are they more numerous but more picturesque.

Utrecht's history is as rich as its accoutrement of canals, mansions, churches, and charitable institutions. It begins in the first century, with the Roman establishment of a military camp, Trajectum ad Rhenum (Ford at the Rhine), in the vicinity of the present cathedral, not far from an arm of the Rhine River. Six centuries later, Dagobert I, King of the Franks, made Utrecht his base from which to attack the Frisians to the north. At the end of the 7th century, the Anglo-Saxon bishop, Willibrord, made Dagobert's stronghold the seat of his bishopric. As Dagobert had set forth from Utrecht to conquer the northern tribes, so Willibrord used the town as his base from which to proselytize and convert. After the Frankish kings came the early Germanic Holy Roman emperors, nominally the rulers of Utrecht. They were wise enough to leave the actual administration of the town in the hands of its prince-archbishops.

Utrecht grew steadily in size and importance particularly beginning in the 12th century, when the small settlement became a town and river commerce brought new prosperity. From the 12th to the 16th century, Utrecht was one of the most powerful feudal cities in the Low Countries. Only in the 16th century did Utrecht begin to lose its dominant political and spiritual position. In 1527, Emperor Charles V incorporated the city into his huge Spanish-Austrian-Burgundian empire. This

Utrecht

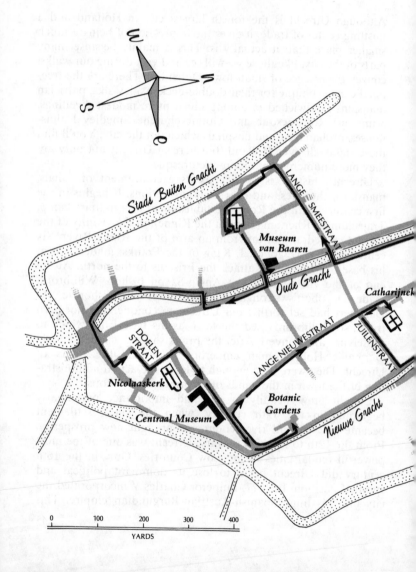

Spanish domination lasted barely fifty years: In 1577, Utrecht revolted and drove out the Spaniards, and two years later joined with six other northern provinces in a treaty called the Union of Utrecht. But by this time the coastal cities of Holland, nourished by trade with the New World, had gained political pre-eminence as well as commercial importance. After the Reformation, the city, once an important Roman Catholic seat, lost its spiritual position as well. The French twice occupied the city: in 1672 to 1674 under Louis XIV, and in 1797 to 1813, during the post–French Revolutionary period and the Napoleonic era. Napoleon appointed his brother Louis Bonaparte King of Holland in 1806. Utrecht regained its status as a Dutch city after 1813 and has since grown steadily as both a commercial and a railway center.

There is so much to see and visit in this lovely city that two walking tours, each a full day in length, are recommended. You might even consider making Utrecht your base for touring Holland, because of its central position. But even if you don't stay in Utrecht, it's so close to Amsterdam, Rotterdam, and The Hague that it's easy to get here to enjoy this city of double-tiered canals, elegant mansions, and medieval almshouses.

Your first walk through Utrecht begins in **Domplein** (Cathedral Square), which was the center of the Roman camp of Trajectum ad Rhenum 2,000 years ago. Today it is the site of a very unusual **cathedral,** which consists only of a choir and a bell tower—its middle portion, the nave, collapsed during a tremendous hurricane which wreaked havoc throughout Utrecht on the first day of August 1674. The nave was never rebuilt, and, what is stranger (considering the proverbial orderliness of the Dutch), the debris after the collapse lay around Domplein for 152 years before being cleared away. Yellow bricks set in the pavement give you an idea of the size of the cathedral prior to the hurricane.

To backtrack a little, the earliest church to occupy this site was built at the end of the 7th century by Bishop Willibrord. He dedicated it to St. Martin, who was later to become patron saint of the town as well. Three centuries later, at the beginning of the 11th century, Bishop Adelbold decided to construct a Romanesque church on the site of the 7th-century foundation. Two centuries after this Romanesque cathedral was completed, Bishop Hendrik van Vianden began construction on an edifice in 1254 which was one of the earliest examples of Gothic style in the Netherlands. This Gothic church did not reach completion until 1517. Then, in 1674, the hurricane struck which wrecked the cathedral's nave.

Ironically, this storm barely touched the cathedral's 364-foot bell tower, which was—and still is—the tallest in Holland. Before visiting the cathedral itself, walk over to this most impressive belfry, called the **Domtoren** (Cathedral Tower). Consisting of two square lower stories and an upper octagonal story, the tower is surmounted by a weather vane in the shape of St. Martin on horseback. The tower houses not only the famous carillon of bells cast by Pierre and François Hemony of Amsterdam in 1663, but also seven early-16th-century bells, one of which, weighing over eight tons, is the second largest in The Netherlands (the largest is in Delft). You can climb to the upper gallery (hours: May to September, daily, 11–3; October to April, weekends, 11–3), from which there is a stupendous view of Utrecht. On a very clear day, you can even see Amsterdam, twenty-six miles to the northwest. To make your climb easier, there are two chapels for you to stop and visit (and rest in) on the way up: the early-14th-century St. Michael's Chapel, with lovely modern stained glass windows, and the Egmond Chapel, named in honor of Bishop George van Egmond, who died in 1549.

Cross over now to visit the cathedral (hours: May to September, Tuesday to Saturday, 2–4). The austerity of the interior is tempered by the beauty of the few modern stained glass windows, but the highlight of this church is the elaborate tomb of Baron van Gendt in the choir. The baron was an energetic gentleman who was not only an admiral of the Dutch navy, but a canon of this cathedral as well. He was killed in battle in 1672, and his tomb was carved by Rombout Verhulst the same year. Nearby in the second chapel on the south side is the tomb of the 13- to 14th-century Bishop Guy van Avesnes and an interesting 15th-century fresco. In the middle of the ambulatory behind the choir is the early-16th-century Holy Sepulcher, once the object of veneration. The crypt holds the hearts of two Holy Roman emperors, Conrad II and Henry V. It was under Henry V in the 12th century that Utrecht grew from a small settlement into a thriving town. The cathedral is frequently used for organ and chamber-music recitals, and you might want to inquire when the next concert is scheduled.

Return to Domplein, where you see two interesting sculptures. The first is a **statue of Count John of Nassau,** the brother of Prince William of Orange, better known as William the Silent, who is one of the heroes of Dutch history. During the 16th century, Holland was part of the vast empire of King Philip II of Spain. Philip's rule was uncompromising and harsh, and it was William who organized his countrymen into resistance and rebellion. William was assassinated in 1584, and was laid to rest in an elaborate sarcophagus in the city in which he died, Delft. Five years before William's death, his brother, John, was instrumental in organizing the seven Protestant northern provinces of the Low Countries into a pact against the Spanish called the Treaty of Utrecht. The nation which was to become the Netherlands grew out of this treaty.

Nearby, just in front of the entrance to the cloister, is a replica of a 10th-century **runic stone** inscribed with characters referring to the Danes' conversion to Christianity. The original of this stone is in Jutland, Denmark, and this replica was presented to the University of Utrecht in 1936 to commemorate two events: the three hundredth anniversary of the founding of the university, and the Danes' conversion to Christianity a thousand years ago. Utrecht was the seat of the first northern bishopric, from which Christianity spread throughout the Netherlands and into Scandinavia.

Before visiting the cloister, walk to the right to No. 29, Utrecht's **University,** founded in 1636 and presently the largest in The Netherlands, with eighteen thousand students. The building you've entered dates only from the end of the last century. Through it you can reach the **Aula,** the Great Auditorium (hours: Monday to Friday, 9–12, 2–5), once the chapter house of the cathedral. Five hundred years ago, the canons of the cathedral used to meet here to discuss matters relating to the day-to-day affairs of their church. The Treaty of Utrecht was signed here in 1579 and the windows bear the coats of arms of the seven provinces which united to resist Spain. The tapestries decorating the walls are recent (1935–1941) and present allegories of the various faculties of the university. As you leave, note the ornate organ with the harpist perched above.

Return now to Domplein near the runic stone and enter the cathedral's former **cloister** (hours: 8 A.M.–sunset), a fine example of late Gothic style. Above the arches are sculptured scenes from the life of St. Martin, who was a Roman officer stationed in Amiens, France, in the first quarter of the 4th century. The story is told that, one blustery winter night, he met a poor old man wandering the streets clad only in scanty rags. Filled with compassion, Martin took off his heavy red soldier's cloak and used his sword to divide it in two, giving one part to the beggar. Asleep that night, Martin dreamed that the beggar he had taken pity on was actually Christ. Soon after that, Martin left the army, was baptized, entered the Church, and eventually became Bishop of Tours. He also became the patron saint of Utrecht. The city's red-and-white coat of arms symbolizes Martin's red soldier's cloak and his later white bishop's robes. In the center of the cloister is a lovely small bronze statuette of a reading monk cast by the Brom brothers in 1913. As you walk around the cloister, notice the Domtoren towering above.

Leave the cloister through the exit on the east side, leading to Achter de Dom (Behind the Cathedral). Across the street at No. 12 are two museums: the **Goud, Zilver en Klokkenmuseum** (Gold, Silver, and Clock Museum) (hours: Monday to Saturday, 10:30–4:30; Sunday, 1:30–4:30) and the museum called **Van Speeldoos tot Pierement** (From Music Boxes to Barrel Organs), a fascinating place displaying "automatic" musical instruments from the 18th century on (hours: Tuesday to Saturday, 11–12, 2–5; Thursday evening at 8). You can hear some of the instruments played if you join a tour.

From these museums, turn left and walk a few steps to Pausdam. To your left is the elegant red brick mansion called **Paushuize** (Pope's House). Built for Adrian Florisze Boeyens in the early 16th century, it received its name when Adrian, who had once served as tutor to the future Charles V, became Pope in 1522. Adrian wasn't Pope for long—he died the following year—but he does have the distinction of being the only Dutch and the last non-Italian Pope.

Walk around the Pope's House along **Kromme Nieuwe Gracht**

(Curving New Canal), which does in fact curve in a semicircle, and is lined with lovely old patrician mansions. Turn left when you come to Pieterstraat, and in a moment you will be in Pieterskerkhof (St. Peter's Churchyard), with the **Pieterskerk** directly ahead. Bernulph, bishop of Utrecht in the second quarter of the 11th century, decided to build this church and three others (St. Mary's, St. John's, and St. Paul's) to surround the cathedral on the east, west, north, and south, forming a cross. Only this church and St. John's remain. During the great hurricane of 1674, the same hurricane which ruined so much of the cathedral, the two west towers and the nave of St. Peter's collapsed, but both were later rebuilt. Since the mid-17th century, this church has been used by Protestant Walloons, the French-speaking peoples of Holland and Belgium. Go inside (hours: Tuesday to Saturday, 10–5) and see the oldest Romanesque-style church in Holland, although the choir is Gothic. The crypt, with its sturdy groined arches, contains the stone sarcophagus of the church's builder, Bishop Bernulph.

Walk through Pieterskerkhof and turn right on Achter St. Pieter (Behind St. Peter). In a few steps, at No. 8, on the corner of Achter St. Pieter and Keistraat, is the ornamented house called the **Huis de Krakeling** (Cracknel, or Biscuit, House), built in the mid-17th century by Edward Meyster. Meyster had a reputation as an eccentric in his day: He is supposed to have habitually stood on one of the high roads leading out of Utrecht, distributing cracknels to wayfarers—it's a pity his descendants didn't continue the custom! Notice the carving on the door and its asymmetrical arch.

Continue along Achter St. Pieter until you come to Korte Jansstraat on the right. This will lead you to **Janskerkhof** (St. John's Churchyard), one of the largest and loveliest of Utrecht's many squares. This one has many fine old trees, and is the scene of a colorful flower market on Saturdays. Directly in front of you is **Janskerk,** another of Bishop Bernulph's Romanesque churches, although this one, twice destroyed by fire, in 1148 and 1279, has very little left that is Romanesque. The present church dates mostly from the early 16th century. At the end of the 17th century, the bell tower and the cloister were pulled down, and in the 250-year period from the end of the 16th century to the beginning of the 19th century, Janskerk served as the city's and then as the university's library. Now it is once again used as a church. If you'd like to have a look at the church's interior, you can apply to the sacristan at No. 26 Janskerkhof.

Surrounding Janskerk are some outstanding examples of domestic architecture from the 16th, 17th, and 18th centuries. Before strolling around the square to see these houses, notice the equestrian statue of Bishop Willibrord near the church. Willibrord is the late-7th-century bishop who came from Northumberland in England to serve as Utrecht's first bishop and to build its first cathedral. In front of the west façade of the church is the statue of Anne Frank, the young Dutch-Jewish heroine of the German occupation during World War II. Anne, who lived in Amsterdam, survived many years living in hiding in an attic with her family. She was finally discovered and deported to a concentration camp, where she met her death. The diary Anne kept during those years of hiding was later discovered and published. The sculpture, representing a young girl with hands clasped behind her back and feet firmly planted on the ground, was completed in 1959 by Pieter d'Hont.

Now take a look at some of the lovely buildings around this square. The fine 18th-century building across the street at No. 10 is one of Utrecht's best hotels. Practically next door, at No. 12, is an elegant 18th-century house now occupied by a bank. Behind the east end of Janskerk is a street bordering a canal called the Drift. Here, at No. 17, is an elegant patrician mansion housing a bank, and up the street at No. 31 is the modest house once occupied by Louis Bonaparte who was created King of Holland in 1806 by his brother Napoleon. Return to Janskerkhof. On the corner at No. 13 is a sumptuous residence built in the mid-17th century, the height of Holland's golden period, decorated with swags of fruit. This building too now houses a bank.

Cross the square to No. 3. This 16th-century building, now part of the university, once belonged to the Order of Minor Friars. Leave Janskerkhof by Korte Jansstraat. Turn right in a few steps into Minrebroederstraat and then right again into Teelingstraat. On the corner of the street called The Hoogt is an interesting 17th-century townhouse with two street fronts, one of which is steeply gabled. Continue straight ahead into

Slachtstraat (Butcher Street), which leads into Jansveld. Halfway up Jansveld, turn left, then left again into Voorstraat. At
No. 19 you pass the building known as the **Grote Vleeshal**
(Large Meat Market), erected in 1637. Butchers were not
allowed to sell meat from their houses (other tradesmen and
sellers of goods were permitted to use their homes for their
businesses), so they banded together to build this market hall,
which is now an antique center. Notice the cow's head above the
doorway. The small, elegant mansion in Renaissance style at
No. 14 is called **De Coninck van Poortugael Huis** (King of
Portugal House) and contains a coin collection (hours: Monday
to Saturday, 9–5:30).

Voorstraat leads into the square called the Neude, dominated
by the huge post–World War I post office. Skirting the post
office on its north side, walk along Potterstraat to **Oude Gracht,**
one of Utrecht's oldest and loveliest canals. The Oude Gracht
was once a branch of the Rhine River and served Utrecht as a
harbor, one long quay where goods were delivered and picked
up. Today you can tour this canal and others by motor launch,
and trips begin at the Viebrug, the bridge directly ahead. Before
leaving Utrecht, take a delightful one-hour cruise through the
heart of the city. Now, however, turn left to walk along the canal
to the corner of Drakenburgstraat and Oude Gracht to see the
Drakenburgh Huis, one of the oldest houses in this city, built in
1328. Cross the bridge and turn right. At No. 99 stop to see **Het
Huis Oudaen,** another of Utrecht's ancient houses. Huis Oudaen
was built in the 14th century for the nobleman Dirc van
Oudaen. In the 17th century, a stone gateway was added and the
mansion was converted into a home for the elderly. Until 1965,
the house continued to serve this function. In 1713, the French
ambassador, Abbé de Polignac, stayed in this house during the
peace negotiations ending the War of the Spanish Succession.
The treaty signed here gave the Netherlands to Charles VI of
Austria, while confirming Philip V as King of Spain. England
benefited from this treaty as well, receiving Gibraltar, New-
foundland, and Nova Scotia.

Turn left into Langeviestraat, lined with large modern shops,
which leads into the mammoth-sized square, the **Vredenburg,**
the center of Utrecht's business district. Twice a year, in March

and September, the Industrial Fair is held here in the Jaar-
beursgebouw (Trade Fair Building), on the west side of the
square. During the 16th century, the Vredenburg castle-fortress,
built by Emperor Charles V, stood in this square. Besides
Holland, Charles numbered Spain, Burgundy, and Austria
among his vast possessions. In 1577, Utrecht revolted, drove out
the Spanish, and demolished the castle, a symbol of Spanish
rule. Today the square is the scene of two colorful markets held
on Saturday, the flea market and the flower market.

Leave the Vredenburg at its southeast end to walk along
Lange Elisabeth Straat. This street like many of the streets in the
area surrounding the Oude Gracht has been reserved for
pedestrians. Walk along and enjoy the variety of shops. At the
fork in the street, go right into Mariastraat, which leads into
Mariaplaats (St. Mary's Place). Across the street is the Gebouw
van Kunsten en Wetenschappen (Society of Arts and Sciences).
St. Mary's, one of the four churches surrounding the cathedral
to form a cross, once stood here. St. Mary's was built by Bishop
Conrad about the year 1080 and was demolished 730 years
later—in the name of progress! All that's left of the Romanesque
church is its **cloister,** which was restored early in this century.
This is a good spot to sit and rest for a few minutes before
continuing your walk.

From Mariaplaats, walk east into Zadelstraat (Saddle Street),
which supposedly takes its name from the slight saddlelike
hump in the middle of the street. Turn left into Donkerstraat to
see the **Huis van Zoudenbalch,** at Nos. 15–19. Built in the middle
of the 15th century by the cathedral's treasurer, Evert van
Zoudenbalch, the mansion once served as an orphanage. Take
the street directly in front of the mansion, Buurkerksteeg, into
Buurkerkhof, where you see the **Buurkerk,** with its great brick
bell tower. In the bricks of this tower you can still see the
indentations made by the cannonballs fired from Vredenburg
Castle in 1577 as the Spaniards made their last defense before
abandoning the city. The church itself dates from the latter half
of the 13th century, although the choir was destroyed in the 16th
century to make way for a new street, appropriately called
Choorstraat (Choir Street). Go inside through the entrance on
Steenweg (hours: Monday to Friday, 12:30–4; Thursday eve-

ning, 7–9) to see the 15th-century frescoes, especially the large one with the Tree of Jesse in the southwest side chapel, and the 16th-century pulpit. Buurkerk is associated with a mystic who called herself Sister Bertken. From the time she was thirty years old until her death, at the age of fifty-seven, Sister Bertken lived in a tiny cell built against the wall of the church. For those twenty-seven years, she abstained from meat and dairy products, went barefoot, and wrote spiritual songs.

From Buurkerk, turn right, then left into Choorstraat, continuing until you come to the **Stadthuis** (City Hall), on the right. This solid-looking building with the Doric columns dates only from 1824, though its cellars go back to the Middle Ages. The reliefs on the façade are the work of Pieter d'Hont, the sculptor of the Anne Frank statue in Janskerkhof, and represent Justice, Watchfulness, Authority, Prudence, and Religion. Turn right from the Stadthuis and walk along **Vismarkt** (Fish Market), with its old fish-market stalls. On Saturday afternoons this is the site of the stamp market.

Turn left on Servetstraat, with the Domtoren in front of you. Just before reaching the bell tower, you pass on the right a gate with the date "1634"; this is all that's left of the bishop's palace. Continue beneath the tower and you are back in Domplein, where you began your walk.

For your second walk through Utrecht, return to Domplein. Walk beneath the Domtoren into Servetstraat until you reach the **Oude Gracht** (Old Canal). In front of you is the Maartensbrug (St. Martin's Bridge). Instead of crossing the bridge, however, turn left and stroll along Lichtegaard and Donkeregaard, which run alongside the canal. Utrecht's canals are unique in Europe, as you may already have noticed—they are far below street level, so that there are two sidewalks, one right alongside the canal, formerly used as a quay or wharf, and another higher up, for pedestrian and street traffic. As you stroll along past typical Dutch houses, be sure to step down once in a while to walk along the quay.

Continue strolling beside the Oude Gracht for about a quarter of a mile, until you come to Korte Smeestraat. Cross the bridge and continue along Lange Smeestraat to No. 40, on the corner, **Bartholomei Gasthuis** (St. Bartholomew's Hospital). This home for the elderly, built by Willem van Abcoude, has been in continuous use for over 550 years. If you love tapestries and have a little patience (you have to wait awhile for someone to show you around), visit its Regents' Room (the Regents were the trustees who administered the hospital), where there are four marvelous 17th-century tapestries, the work of Maximiliaan van der Gucht of Delft.

Turn left along Pelmolenweg to the 13th-century Geertekerk (St. Gertrude's Church). Skirt the outside of the church to reach the Geertestraat, directly behind. Straight ahead is the Oude Gracht. Make a short detour to the left to visit the **Museum van Baaren,** at No. 317 (hours: Tuesday, Wednesday, and Thursday, 10:30–3:30), a lovely mansion where you can browse through an interesting collection of paintings. The van Baarens, brother and sister, both of whom died not many years ago, accumulated a valuable collection, which includes an early Mondrian, several van Goghs, and numerous other Dutch artists of the late 19th and early 20th centuries. If possible, ask your concierge to call in advance to say you're coming; otherwise, just ring the bell and ask to see the paintings.

From the museum, turn right and cross the **Geertebrug,** with its carved figures on either side—facing south is a medieval wayfarer, and facing north is St. Gertrude, who dispensed food and drink to weary travelers. Turn right and walk one block to Eligenstraat. Attached with chains to the wall of the house on the corner is a boulder called *de gesloten steen,* the chained stone. There is a legend that, if the stone were not chained, the devil would toss it back and forth from the Geertebrug to the Vollersbrug (the next bridge south) in a devilish game of catch—but who would be on the other bridge to catch the stone and toss it back, the legend does not say.

Cross the Vollersbrug and walk along the opposite bank of the Oude Gracht. To your right you pass the **statue of St. Martin on horseback** carved by A. Termote. Martin is not only the city's patron saint, but also the province's. Continue to the end of Oude Gracht, turn left, cross the bridge, and walk along

Tolsteegbarriere and Wijde Doelen. When you come to Schut-
terstraat (Marksman Street), turn left and then right to visit No.
12 Doelenstraat. A small 17th-century doorway leads to a
cloister, which was once part of the medieval monastery
connected with Nicolaaskerk (St. Nicholas). In the 17th century
the buildings were used as a prison, and they became an
almshouse in 1898. Continue ahead on Doelenstraat to Nic-
olaasdwarsstraat. Turn left to No. 2, six rent-free dwellings
established in the middle of the 17th century by Jan van
Gronsvelt to shelter poor families. Utrecht is full of such small
picturesque houses erected during the Middle Ages to shelter
the poor, the elderly, and orphans or to care for the sick. On
today's walk you will pass many other examples of medieval
charitable institutions. These particular houses in front of you
were moved to this site in 1756. Across the street is the Van de
Poll workhouse, dating from the early 17th century. Finally, turn
right into Nicolaaskerkhof to visit the Romanesque **Nicolaaskerk.** Most of the church dates from the mid-12th century.
One of the Romanesque bell towers houses a carillon of twenty-
three bells made by the Hemony brothers in 1654.

From Nicolaaskerk turn right along Agnietenstraat. At No. 1
is Utrecht's **Centraal Museum** (hours: Tuesday to Saturday, 10–
5; Sunday, 2–5; closed Monday), which is actually two separate
museums (municipal and archiepiscopal), housed in the 15th-
century convent of St. Agnes. Begin your visit in the 16th-
century chapel just off the vestibule, which houses the oldest
collection of **stations of the cross** in Holland, thirteen stone
carvings from the 14th-century church of Aalten, a town in
eastern Holland close to the German border. Opposite the
chapel are several rooms, the second of which contains the
paintings of Jan van Scorel and other artists of the so-called
Utrecht School. Jan van Scorel, a native of Alkmaar, spent
many years in the first half of the 16th century painting in
Utrecht. He introduced what is known as the Italianate style into
Dutch art, and the school which grew up around him imitated
this style. Notice his *Deposition from the Cross* (1540). His
masterpieces are the thirty-eight portraits, painted between 1525
and 1541, entitled *Pilgrims of Jerusalem,* depicting various
members of a group called the Brotherhood of Jerusalem

(consisting of pilgrims who had journeyed to the Holy Land). The artist included himself among the pilgrims (see the lower group, left side—the artist is the fifth from the right). Just beyond this room are the **Stijlkamers,** model rooms taken from old Utrecht houses and decorated in styles appropriate to the 15th through the mid-19th centuries. One of the period rooms displays a marvelous Poppenhuis (Doll's House), a miniature of a rich merchant's home of the late 17th century.

Return to the foyer to visit Rooms 6, 7, and 8, where you can view an excellent collection of medieval art, sculpture, reliquaries, and illuminated manuscripts. Don't miss the collection of **medieval codices,** including one attributed to Bishop Bernulph, displayed in the cases in Room 7.

Finally, go up to the first floor. Rooms 10 to 15 contain the paintings of numerous 17th-century artists, including several of Utrecht's native sons: Hendrick Bloemaert, Jan Both, Jan de Heem, Gerard van Honthorst, and Cornelis van Poelenburgh.

Right next door to the Centraal Museum, at No. 5 Agnietenstraat, is the **Fondatie van Renswoude,** one of several institutions in this vicinity which cared for orphans, the sick, or the elderly. The Van Renswoude Foundation with its impressive rococo façade was begun in 1757 by Maria Duyst van Voorhout, the Baroness van Renswoude, to care for orphaned children. The Foundation has a Regents' Room, where the trustees of the Foundation used to meet, and several of their group portraits are nearby. Portraits like these were extremely popular in 17th- and 18th-century Holland, and many of the great artists of the day, including Rembrandt and Frans Hals, were commissioned to paint group portraits. Ring the bell if you're interested in taking a look. Across the street, on the corner of Agnietenstraat and Lange Nieuwstraat, is **Beyerskameren** (Beyers Almshouses), founded in 1597 by Adriaan Beyer for poor old people. Next door to Beyerskameren on Agnietenstraat is a group of twelve tiny houses, the **Fondatie Maria van Pallaes,** which were built in 1651 by Maria van Pallaes to house poor women.

A few steps beyond this almshouse is Utrecht's **Botanic Gardens,** with an entrance at No. 185 Nieuwe Gracht (hours: Monday to Friday, 9–12, 1:30–5). This small area, part of the University of Utrecht, has a variety of greenhouses filled with tropical plants, cacti, and succulents. After you've looked around, return to Lange Nieuwstraat and turn right past the Beyerskameren. Walk along this street past Catharijnekerk (St. Catherine's) to No. 34, **Kleine Vleeshal** (Small Meat Market), which was established in 1432. This meat market, like the Grote Vleeshal which you saw on your first walk through Utrecht, was built by the butchers of the area who were not permitted to sell meat directly from their homes. Notice the appropriate cow's head above the front door.

Return to the **Catharijnekerk,** Utrecht's Roman Catholic cathedral. Begun in the mid-15th century by the Carmelites, it was completed one hundred years later by the Knights of St. John and has the distinction of being the last Gothic church built in Utrecht.

Return to Lange Nieuwstraat and turn left on Zuilenstraat, where there are several fine old patrician mansions. In front of you is another one of Utrecht's canals with double-decker sidewalks, the **Nieuwe Gracht** (New Canal). Turn left to stroll beside this lovely canal, lined with picturesque 18th-century houses. Past Hamburgerstraat, look for the short street called the Hofpoort with a gateway dating from the early 17th century. This was once the area where Utrecht's law courts were located, and there are still a lot of law offices here. Walk along Hofpoort for a moment in this secluded corner of the city. Return to Hamburgerstraat and cross the bridge. Then turn right to walk . along the canal to Brigittenstraat on the left. At the end of Brigittenstraat, turn right along Lepelenburg. Just to your right along this street is a group of a dozen almshouses, the **Bruntenhof,** founded in 1621 by Frederik Brunt to shelter elderly women. These houses are among the most charming of Utrecht's generous array of orphanages and almshouses.

Lepelenburg becomes Servaasbolwerk, and after a few feet you will come to **Leeuwenbergh Hospital** on the right. In 1567, Agnes van Leeuwenbergh gave this hospital to Utrecht for the care of plague victims. Since then it has served as a barracks, a chemical laboratory, and, nowadays, as a church. Take the street which curves to the left directly across from the hospital and go over the first bridge you come to. If you turned left and walked along Maliebann, a wide tree-lined boulevard, for about a quarter of a mile, you would come to Utrecht's **Museum of Modern Art** (No. 42), which has a good collection of paintings from the mid-19th century to the present day (hours: Monday to Saturday, 10–5; Sunday, 2–5). From the bridge, however, continue straight ahead on Johan van Oldenbarneveltlaan to the **Spoorwegmuseum,** the Netherlands Railway Museum. Housed in a former railway station, it shelters trains from the early 19th century on (hours: Tuesday to Saturday, 10–5; Sunday, 1–5; closed Monday). Behind the building are eight steam locomotives, dated 1839 to 1945. Here among the retired engines and railway cars and the operating model trains is where you end your second walk through Utrecht.

SPAIN

AVILA

Avila sits atop a ridge, in the midst of a rock-strewn, treeless plain, a city almost forgotten by the passing centuries. Once known as *"la ciudad de cantos y santos"*—the city of stones and saints—Avila still lives up to its name, although its days of grandeur are long past. The stones are still abundantly present— in the mighty medieval walls which completely encircle the old city, in the massive fortresslike cathedral, in the narrow, crooked streets—but today they are forlorn reminders of the greatness which once belonged to this city. The saints who once lived within these walls, worshiped in the cathedral, and trod the narrow streets, are also long gone, but they have imparted something of their mystical air to temper the austere melancholy of this ancient city.

Avila's history stretches a long way back. There is evidence within the old walled city of the ancient Iberian civilization which once flourished here. Known as Avela, the city was one of the outposts of the Roman Empire; it was christianized by St. Segundo in the middle of the first century. After the Romans came the hordes of Visigoths from the north who overran all of the Iberian peninsula. In the middle of the eighth century, the Moors from north Africa also invaded the area, before penetrating into France. For 350 years, the town seesawed between Moors and Spaniards, until final reconquest by Raimundo de Borgoña in 1090. Avila's next claim to fame came four centuries later, with Theresa of Jesus, one of the great mystics of the 16th century and one of Spain's greatest saints. The Jews were expelled in the late 15th century, as were the Moriscos, descendents of the Moorish invaders, a century later. With the departure of these two groups began Avila's decline as an economic power and her subsequent decay into a brooding shadow of her former self.

Today, the memory of Avila's past glory is very much with you as you stroll through this lovely, sad city through streets lined with once-aristocratic residences, past numerous Roman-

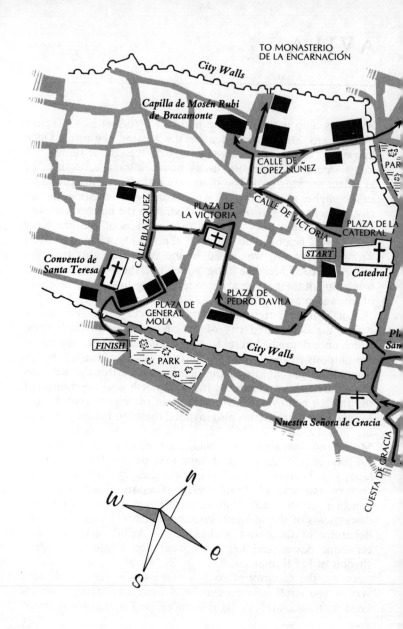

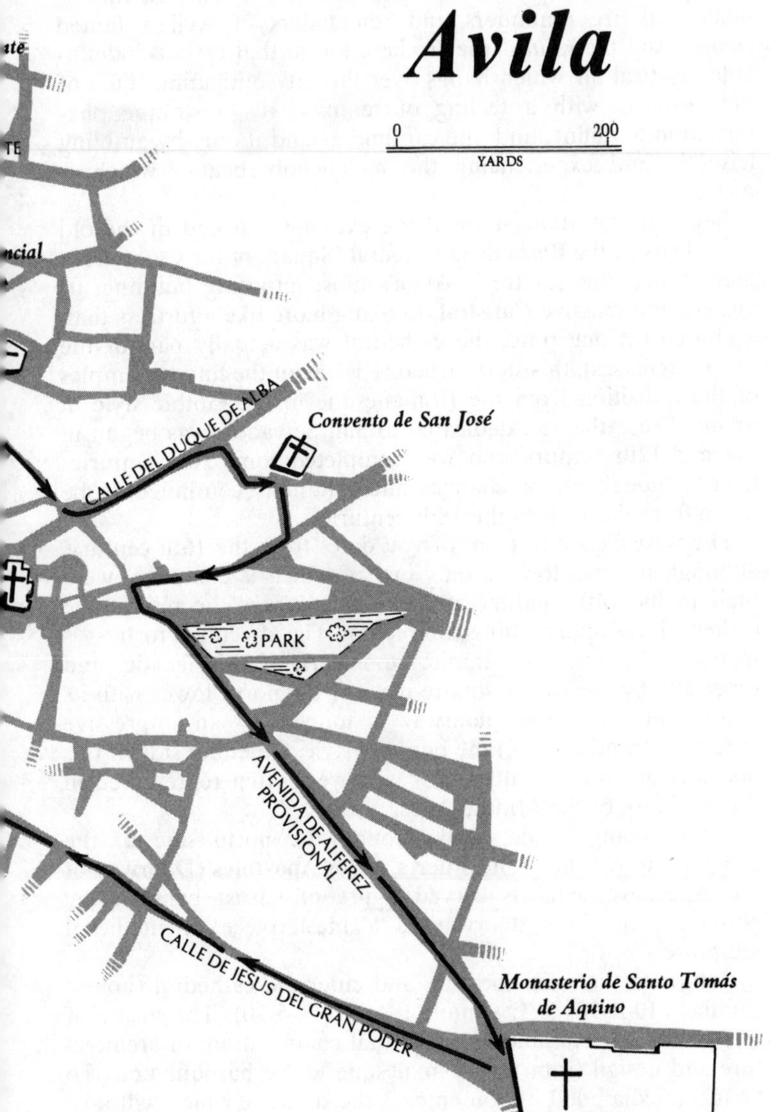

Avila

0   200

YARDS

ue

TE

ncial

CALLE DEL DUQUE DE ALBA

Convento de San José

PARK

AVENIDA DE ALFEREZ
PROVISIONAL

CALLE DE JESÚS DEL GRAN PODER

*Monasterio de Santo Tomás
de Aquino*

esque-Gothic churches, and beside the ancient stone walls, perhaps the most perfect testimonial to the city's past importance. All are reminders and remainders of Avila's famed *cantos.* And the *santos*—they're here too in that certain indefinable mystical air which hangs over this city mitigating some of the austerity with a feeling of serenity. It's a strange phenomenon to define, and one can understand it only by ambling leisurely and experiencing the melancholy beauty which is Avila.

Begin your walking tour at the extreme east end of the old walled city in the **Plaza de la Catedral** (Square of the Cathedral). Dominating this square is Avila's most imposing building, its austere and massive **Catedral.** Looking more like a fortress than a church (at one time, the cathedral was actually part of the town's defenses), this stern structure is one of the finest examples of the transition from the Romanesque to the Gothic style in Spain. The cathedral, dedicated to San Salvador, was begun in the mid-12th century and was completed some two centuries later, although major changes and additions continued to be made from the 15th to the 18th centuries.

The west façade in front of you dates from the 16th century, although the two towers, only one of which is complete, were built in the 14th century at the same time as the rest of the cathedral was approaching completion. The effect of a fortress is increased by the gray granite stonework of this façade, and especially by the sturdy square mass of the north tower with its battlements. The **west doorway** is topped by an impressive limestone frontispiece in the baroque style. On either side of this doorway are stone "wild men," who were often represented in the sculpture of the Middle Ages.

Before going inside, walk around the north side of the cathedral to see the grand **Puerta de los Apóstoles** (Doorway of the Apostles), with its carved figure of Christ beneath the pointed arch. This doorway is a masterpiece of medieval sculpture.

Return to the west doorway and enter the cathedral (hours: summer, 10–1:30, 3–7; winter, 10–1:30, 3–5:30). The inside of this proud, ancient church is a virtual compendium of architecture and design from the Romanesque to the baroque eras. To your immediate left as you enter is the staircase which will take you to the top of the 14th-century north tower for a lovely view over the town and the surrounding Castilian landscape. Along this north side of the cathedral are also some lovely Renaissance chapels; the first two are enclosed by impressive wrought-iron grilles. Just outside the first chapel is a 15th-century **baptismal font,** an example of fine German workmanship. The base of the font is the work of the early-16th-century sculptor Vasco de la Zarza.

Walk toward the **trascoro** (behind the choir area) to see the 16th-century bas-reliefs. Now walk along the south side; on the other side of the trascoro is the choir, with its Renaissance **stalls** carved by the Dutch artisan Cornelius in 1536. These carvings represent scenes from the lives of various saints. The alabaster altars just beyond the choir to the right and left are also products of the Renaissance. They are carved with incidents from the lives of two of the city's patron saints, Segundo and Catherine.

In front of you is the magnificent **Capilla Major,** the sanctuary partially enclosed by a grille, containing the cathedral's main altar. Over the altar is the remarkable **reredos** (altar screen) representing scenes from the life of Christ, painted between 1499 and 1508 by three of the most famous and influential artists of the early Renaissance in Spain, Pedro Berruguete, Juan de Borgoña, and Santa Cruz.

In the south transept are several 16th-century tombs, as well as the entrance to the cathedral's sacristy and museum. The sacristy is a vaulted room with an alabaster altar decorated with bas-reliefs by Vasco de la Zarza and his pupils. The museum adjacent is a treasurehouse of sculptures, paintings, and gold- and silverwork. The highlight of this collection is the huge six-foot monstrance created by Juan de Arfe in 1564.

Behind the Capilla Major you find the monumental alabaster **tomb** of Bishop Alonso de Madrigal, who died in 1455; he was nicknamed *"el Tostado,"* "the toasted." The legend says that the good bishop's cloak once caught fire as he was sitting beside a brazier, unconcernedly writing away, hence, the nickname—"the toasted"; it's a good thing it wasn't "the fried." A more mundane explanation for this nickname may be the bishop's swarthy complexion. The tomb itself is another example of the artistry of Vasco de la Zarza. It was completed in 1518.

You are in the apse, the oldest part of the cathedral,

completed in Romanesque style in the 12th century and imbedded in the old town wall. Notice the thickness of the walls here.

Before leaving, be sure to visit the cathedral's 14th-century Gothic **cloister.** Spend a few minutes sitting or strolling in this serene, secluded corner.

Leave the cathedral by the west door. On the left side of the Plaza de la Catedral is the 14th-century Palacio Valderrabanos, now the city's best hotel. To the right is the **Palacio del Marqués de Velada,** once the mansion of the powerful and aristocratic Velada family. Holy Roman Emperor Charles V, grandson of Ferdinand and Isabella and King of Spain from 1516 to 1558, resided here for a short time in the early 16th century. The mansion is characteristic of many of Avila's aristocratic residences. Its exterior is massive and somber, conveying a sense of melancholia, a feeling which is dispelled after entering the interior patio. It's almost as if the house is hiding its gay heart behind an austere façade.

Past the Palacio, bear to the left along Calle Tomás Luis de Victoria until you come to the Plaza de Zurraquín. Turn right into Calle de Bracamonte, which leads you to Plaza de Mosén Rubi, with the imposing **Capilla de Mosén Rubi de Bracamonte** on the left side of the square. This chapel, built in 1516, is now the home of a Dominican convent. It is an unusual blending of Gothic and Renaissance styles, and houses the sarcophagus of its founders, the Bracamonte family. Walk inside to see the tomb and the 16th-century stained glass (if the church is not open, ask to be admitted at the convent to the left).

Return to Plaza de Mosén Rubi and turn left into the adjacent Plaza Fuente del Sol. The mansion at the far end, closest to the City Walls, belonged to the Bracamontes. Next door is the **Palacio de los Aguilas,** the former home of the Aguilas family. This mansion, like the Palacio del Marqués de Velada, which you saw earlier, wears a severe façade with little ornamentation. The main entrance is at No. 2, but this large house extends to the corner. At the corner take Calle de Lopez Nuñez. The lovely mansion at No. 1 on the left has an attractive classical doorway. Across the street (No. 4) is the massive **Palacio de los Verdugo,** the former residence of the Verdugo family. Its forbidding exterior is mitigated by the twin corner turrets and the coats of arms over the windows and doorway. The courtyard contains an excellent example of an Iberian stone bull, a remnant from Avila's pre-Roman days.

Continue along Calle de Lopez Nuñez to the **Puerta de San Vicente** (St. Vincent's Gateway), one of the most handsome of the nine gateways of the old town. This ancient gate, dating from the late 11th century, consists of two high towers joined by a very high arch (which you can see from the other side). Walk beneath the gate, leaving behind you the oldest part of the city of Avila, that part enclosed by the 11th-century walls.

To the left of the gate across the square is one of Avila's most interesting transitional Romanesque-Gothic churches, **San Vicente** (St. Vincent). It was supposedly erected on the site where St. Vincent and his two sisters, Sabina and Cristeta, met their martyrdom in the 4th century. Begun in the late 12th century by Master Fruchel, also the first architect of the cathedral, the building of this church spanned the 12th, 13th, and 14th centuries. This was the era which witnessed the change from Romanesque to Gothic style, a style heralded by Fruchel, who is credited with being the first to introduce Gothic architecture into Spain. Walk along the south side beneath the unfinished 13th-century portico to the **south door.** This 12th-century masterpiece is ornamented with the sculptured figures of King David and Sabina on the right and the Annunciation on the left.

Return to the red sandstone west façade to examine the 13th-century **doorway,** whose pillars bear the statues of the Apostles. Enter the church through this doorway and walk down the main aisle to the transept crossing to view the magnificent 12th-century **tomb** of St. Vincent and his sisters. It is borne on graceful, slender columns and rests beneath an elaborate 15th-century baldachin. The carvings on the sarcophagus depict the martyrdom of the three saints. At the end of the north aisle is a stairway leading to a **crypt** containing a much-venerated 12th-century image called the Virgin de la Soterrana (Subterranean Virgin). Here also you can see the rock on which Vincent, Sabina, and Cristeta supposedly suffered martyrdom in the year 303.

From San Vicente, turn left and walk across the park which faces the Puerta San Vicente to the Calle de Eduardo Marquina in the far corner. After one block, turn right on Calle de Arturo Dupirier. The **Museo Provincial,** Avila's Provincial Museum, is to your left on Plaza de Nalvillos. Inside (hours: Tuesday to Saturday, 10–2, 6–8; Sunday, 11–1:30; closed Monday) is an interesting collection of paintings, statues, and sarcophagi from all periods of Avila's history.

Cross the Plaza de Nalvillos and walk past the church of Santo Tomé. In the Plaza de Italia, bear left across the square into Calle de D. Ferreol Hernandez. Turn left on Calle del Duque de Alba, then right on Calle del Padre Silverio. In a few minutes, you will reach the **Convento de San José** (Convent of St. Joseph), which has the distinction of being the first of the eighteen convents founded by St. Theresa in the years between 1562 and 1582. The church as you see it today dates from the early years of the 17th century and contains some outstanding paintings from the Madrilenian (Madrid) School of the late 17th century. Go inside (hours: 9–2, 3–6) to see the reredos, *The Assumption,* painted in 1608 by Pantoja de la Cruz. It's located in the third chapel on the north side of the church.

Take the street directly across from the main entrance of the church, Calle de las Madres. Turn right on Calle de San Juan de la Cruz and left on Calle de Sor Maria de San José for one short block. Then turn left, downhill along Avenida de Alferez Provisional. You pass a park on your left from which there is a fine view of the surrounding countryside. After a brisk ten-minute walk, you will come to the **Monasterio de Santo Tomás de Aquino** (Monastery of St. Thomas Aquinas). The monastery possesses a fine late-Gothic church erected at the close of the 15th century by the Catholic monarchs Ferdinand and Isabella, shortly after the death of their only son, Juan. These two monarchs are noted for their success in uniting Spain through their marriage, driving out the Moors, and financing Columbus's voyages to the New World.

The interior (hours: summer, 10–12, 8–9; Sunday, 9–1, 8–9) consists of a single aisle flanked by chapels. Walk directly to the transept to see the magnificent alabaster **tomb** of Juan, heir to the throne of Ferdinand and Isabella and brother of Catherine of Aragon (the first wife of Henry VIII of England), who died in 1497, at the age of nineteen. The lifelike replica of the young prince was carved by the Florentine sculptor Domenico Fancelli in 1512.

Beneath the vaulted ceiling is the high altar, resplendent with a **retable** depicting the life of St. Thomas Aquinas painted about 1500 by Pedro Berruguete. Visit the three fine two-story **cloisters,** especially the one called "de los Reyes" (of the Kings). It was constructed for Ferdinand and Isabella as their summer court, but after Juan's death they didn't remain in Avila long. Somewhere near this courtyard rest the remains of Tomás de Torquemada, the first and most famous of the Grand Inquisitors, who died in 1498. Torquemada was also the founder of this monastery. The Inquisition as it existed in Spain was established by Pope Sixtus IV at the request of Ferdinand and Isabella. Although it was ostensibly set up to root out religious heresy, it often served as a political tool and, in addition, was often pursued with cruelty and severity. The exact location of Torquemada's tomb is unknown. He was first buried in the monastery's chapter house, now the sacristy, but the tomb was destroyed in the 19th century.

Leave the church and take the street straight ahead, Calle de Jesus del Gran Poder (Street of the Almighty Jesus). After a walk of about ten minutes, you will reach a stepped street on your right, Cuesta de Gracia. Bear left, and as you walk up, to your left is the **Convento de Nuestra Señora de Gracia** (Convent of Our Lady of Grace), where the child who was to become St. Theresa was educated. Turn left again beyond the convent. When you reach the top, turn right on Bajada a Sonsoles beside the town walls, which will bring you to the Plaza de Santa Teresa. The church of **San Pedro** (St. Peter) is here, a lovely saffron pink structure begun in the Romanesque period and completed in the Gothic, like many of Avila's churches. The church is noted for its rose window, cupola, and three round-arched doorways. The **west door** is considered one of the masterpieces of Romanesque art in Spain.

Walk inside to see one of the church's masterpieces, located in the north transept, a Virgin and Saints **retable** by the late-15th-century artist Juan de Borgoña.

From San Pedro walk directly ahead into Plaza de Santa Teresa, a lively square lined with cafés. In the early evening hours this square is also the site of the *paseo,* or evening stroll, when natives and tourists alike gather to walk and chat before dinner. In front of you is another of the old town's remarkable gateways, **Puerta del Alcázar** (Gateway of the Alcazar, or Castle), which still incorporates some of the original Roman masonry of two thousand years ago. This gateway, like the Puerta de San Vicente, consists of two enormous towers joined by a high arch. If you like, you can climb (steep steps) a section of the walls, of which the gateway is a part. The entrance is adjacent to the gateway on the left inside (hours: 11:30–1, 4:30–6:30).

Walk through the gateway into the Plaza de Calvo Sotelo, and cross this square into Calle del Generalisimo Franco, named in honor of Spain's former head of government. Turn left into Plaza del Teniente Arevalo. Cross the square and take the street which leads out on the left, Calle del Cardenal Plá y Deniel. This soon leads into the small Plaza de Pedro Davila. On the left side of the square is a series of ancient buildings once belonging to the noble Davila family. Built over five hundred years ago, they display a uniformly severe façade and battlements.

Turn right on Calle de Caballeros (Street of Gentlemen) and walk to the lovely arcaded square, **Plaza de la Victoria** (Square of Victory). This is Avila's main square, the center of life and activity in the Old Town today, as it has been for centuries. On the south side is the late-16th-century church of **San Juan** (St. John). Just inside the entrance, on the north side, is the baptismal font in which St. Theresa was baptized as an infant in 1515.

From San Juan, walk directly ahead on Calle de Blasco Gimeno. At the corner, note the modern structures with their balconies, a pleasant contrast to the numerous ancient buildings you've been seeing. Turn right past this building into Calle Jimena Blazquez and, in a few steps, just across the street you see the **Palacio de Polentinos,** built in 1520 by Vasco de la Zarza who also designed El Tostado's sarcophagus in the cathedral. This mansion is an outstanding example of the Plateresque style in Spanish architecture, which dates from the reign of Ferdinand and Isabella. The Plateresque or "silver-plate" style incorporates many Moorish elements and features rich, delicate ornamentation. The central, highly decorated doorway and inner patio of this mansion are lovely examples of this style. The building is presently occupied by the Academy of Logistics.

Retrace your steps down Calle Blazquez. Turn left on Calle de Marcelino Santiago, continuing until you come to the Plaza de General Mola. On the left side of the square is one of Avila's most beautiful mansions, **Palacio del Conde de Oñate** (Palace of the Count of Oñate), with its tall, proud, battlemented tower. This noble tower is called **Torre de los Guzmanes** (Tower of the Cadets). Across the street is the **Palacio de Superunda,** a mansion in classical style. Turn right, and next door to the Palacio de Superunda is the 16th-century **Palacio de Almarza,** the former home of the aristocratic Almarza family; across from this mansion, there is yet another handsome though modern building.

Continue walking to the Plaza de la Santa (Square of the Saint). On the right side of this square is the **Convento de Santa Teresa,** with the baroque church built over the site of the saint's birthplace. Theresa is a fascinating saint: Born in 1515 into the aristocratic Cepeda y Ahumada family, she grew up surrounded by twelve brothers and sisters. Because of her parents' social status, she received an education at the Convento de Nuestra Señora de Gracia which we passed by earlier, just beneath the walls of the Old Town. Theresa was beautiful, humorous, and wealthy, but, at the age of eighteen, she decided to renounce her wealth and position and enter the Carmelite Convento de la Encarnación (Convent of the Incarnation) just north of the city. In her first ten years at this convent, Theresa was not overly strict with her religious vows, but this changed radically when her father died when she was 28. At the age of forty, Theresa began to experience trances and visions. Although blessed with mystic powers, she managed to retain her humor and carefree attitude toward life. One of her favorite sayings was "God deliver me from sullen saints." At about this time, Theresa decided to reform her religious order, the Carmelites, and for the last twenty years of her life she traveled barefoot throughout the Spanish countryside, accompanied by another great Spanish mystic, Juan de la Cruz (John of the Cross) preaching poverty and penitence. They founded monasteries and convents where a stricter rule of religious life would be observed.

One of the most famous stories told about Theresa during her journeys throughout Spain is the one in which she very nearly drowned while crossing a flooded river near Burgos. She berated the Lord for her near disaster, and He replied: "This is how I treat my friends." Theresa's retort was: "Yes, and that is why Thou hast so few friends." This woman who lived four hundred years ago seems very human with her sense of humor and healthy skepticism.

Go inside the baroque memorial (hours: 10–1:30, 3–7; closes one hour earlier in winter). The spot where Theresa supposedly was born is now marked by an elaborate baroque-style chapel with a statue of her wearing a golden crown. Theresa, who spent 20 years preaching poverty and trodding the countryside shoeless, would have laughed at it! Not quite so laughable is a relic of the saint preserved in a room near where the postcards are sold (left side of the square as you leave the church): her finger covered with rings. After Theresa's burial, her body was exhumed and dismembered, and parts of it were sent to various churches that wanted "mementos"—God deliver her from morbid admirers!

To your left is the **Palacio Marques de Benevites,** now a museum and library (hours: 10–12, 4–6) housing mementos and writings of the saint. Across the square from the museum is another aristocratic residence, the 15th-century **Casa de Nuñez Vela,** with its lovely classical inner patio.

In front of the church is the massive gateway, **Puerta de Santa Teresa.** Walk through it, and before you is a lovely view of the Ambles Valley and the mountains just beyond. Off to your left is the Romanesque church of Santiago (St. James), with its tall 14th-century tower.

As you stand here, one of the highlights of this lovely city is just behind you, the **Murallas** (Walls) which completely surround the medieval town. These walls are Romanesque in design and were built between 1090 and 1099 by Count Raimondo de Borgoña on the instructions of his father-in-law, the Castilian King Alfonso VI. Their construction coincided with Avila's complete victory over the Moorish invaders, who were finally routed after three and a half centuries of seesaw struggle. These walls are one of the masterpieces of medieval military architecture. They consist of forty-foot-high, ten-foot-thick walls interspersed with eighty-eight sturdy granite towers and pierced by nine gateways. They encircle (or en-box, since they form a rectangle) the city on all sides, for a distance of a mile and a half. These Murallas, the finest and oldest in Spain, are among the best preserved city walls in Europe. If you don't feel like walking around them, take your car or hire a taxi and drive around the outside. It's a must!

For now, walk to your left to the park overlooking the valley. From here you have a good view over the land below, as well as a magnificent view of the Murallas, and there is no better place in which to end your stroll through this city of saints and stones.

* * *

Before leaving Avila, you should try to walk or drive to the **Monasterio de la Encarnación** (Monastery of the Incarnation). It's only three-quarters of a mile from the Puerta San Vicente, just north of the town. The convent itself was founded by the Carmelites in 1499, sixteen years before Theresa was born. In 1533, when she was eighteen, Theresa joined the order, and she lived here for the next thirty years. Inside the convent (hours: 9:30–1:30, 3:30–7; closes 1½ hours earlier in winter), you can see some of the rooms in which Theresa spent so much of her life, as well as her manuscripts and relics. There is an interesting contemporary drawing of Theresa done by the other great Avilan saint, San Juan de la Cruz, her companion during the latter part of her life.

Finally, for a really spectacular view over all of Avila, drive over the Puente Nuevo (New Bridge), which crosses the River Adaja just outside the western walls of the Old Town. Bear to the right, following the signs to Salamanca. After a short distance, you will come to a cross between four columns, **Los Cuatro Postes** (The Four Pillars), from which you have a fabulous view of Avila. Return at night, when the walls are lit and seem unreal. It's like something from a dream about the Middle Ages, complete with castles and knights.

SEVILLE

Ornately grilled windows, balconies overlooking sunny, narrow streets, patios with bubbling fountains and pots of flowers, orange and palm trees, Moorish towers—all have come to symbolize Seville, Andalusia's principal city. Seville is a city which mixes fact and fantasy easily: The numerous Mudejar (Spanish-Moorish) towers, churches, and mansions testify to the city's past grandeur and importance as part of Moslem Spain and later under the medieval and Renaissance Spanish monarchs. But Seville is equally the city of Don Juan and Carmen, of warm nights with the scent of orange blossoms in the air, of *señoritas* in flouncy, brightly colored dresses, and of flamenco music in the early hours of the morning. And it is precisely this blend of fact and fantasy which makes Seville such an exciting, gay city. The excitement peaks twice a year: during Holy Week preceding Easter Sunday, when the entire city assumes an air of penitence and pageantry and elaborate *pasos* (floats) are carried through the city in procession, and during the April Fair, shortly after Easter, when the city becomes one huge festival with parades, horse shows, and bullfights. Try to visit Seville during Holy Week and/or April Fair; but, if you do, be sure to arrive a few days before the festivities begin so you can take the walking tours before the city becomes crowded.

Numerous different peoples have made Seville their home. The Phoenicians established a fortress and trading post here; the Romans under Julius Caesar conquered the city, renamed it Hispalis, and made it a regional capital. In the turbulent 5th century, both Vandals and Visigoths stormed through and, in 712, Moslem tribes invaded from North Africa and remained to rule for more than five hundred years. At first the chief port under the centuries-long dominance of Cordoba, Seville became the principal city of Moslem Spain after the fall of Cordoba in the 11th century. The great age of Moorish building, which produced the Alcázar, the Tower of Gold, the defense walls, and the mosques, was during the 12th and early 13th centuries. In

1248, King Ferdinand III of Castile conquered the city. A century later, Pedro the Cruel made Seville his favored residence, and the 15th-century Catholic monarchs Ferdinand and Isabella, who united Spain by their marriage, ruled from here for a time. But Seville's "golden age" coincided with Spain's exploration of the New World during the entire 16th century. It was the age in which Magellan circumnavigated the globe and Pizarro and Cortez discovered the riches of Mexico and South America for Spain. Seville's decline as a center of power began in the mid-17th century, when trade and commerce began moving toward Cadiz and especially when Spain began to lose, little by little, her vast colonial empire.

So much grandeur and elegance still survives from Seville's glorious Moorish, medieval, and Renaissance past that two walks, each requiring a full day, are suggested. If you have scheduled one day for Seville, take the first walk, which encompasses most of the city's important sights. The second walk centers around some of Seville's numerous churches and mansions and takes you to various sections of the city. However, be sure to allow a little time to linger in this spectacular city, one of the most important in Spain for almost a thousand years, and discover those secluded corners and shady patios which so evoke the essence of Seville and its incomparable past.

Begin your first walk through Seville at the **Cathedral.** This impressive Gothic structure is the largest church in Spain and the third largest in the world (after St. Peter's in Rome and St. Paul's in London). Occupying the site of an ancient Moslem mosque, the cathedral was begun in 1402, and its construction continued over the entire 15th century. It stands as a monument to the architectural genius of that era, and houses innumerable examples of superb art and craftsmanship.

In front of you is the cathedral's main entrance, the **Puerta Mayor** (Main Door), decorated with Apostles on either side and the Assumption of the Virgin into Heaven in the tympanum. To the right is the Puerta del Nacimiento (Door of the Nativity), and to the left is the Puerta del Bautismo (Door of the Baptism). Both doors are adorned with fine 15th-century statues.

After examining these three grand portals, enter the cathedral (hours: 10:30–1, 4–7 in summer) through the Puerta Mayor.

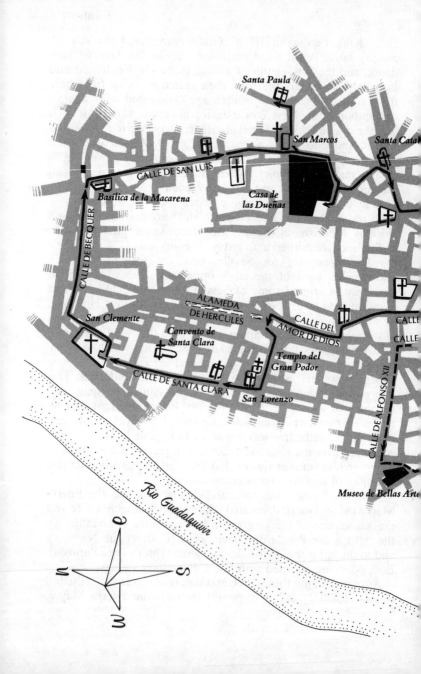

Santa Paula

San Marcos

Santa Cata

CALLE DE SAN LUIS

Basilica de la Macarena

Casa de
las Dueñas

CALLE DE BECQUER

ALAMEDA
DE HERCULES

CALLE DEL
AMOR DE DIOS

CALLE

San Clemente

Convento de
Santa Clara

Templo del
Gran Podor

CALLE

CALLE DE SANTA CLARA

San Lorenzo

CALLE DE ALFONSO XII

Museo de Bellas Arte

Rio Guadalquivir

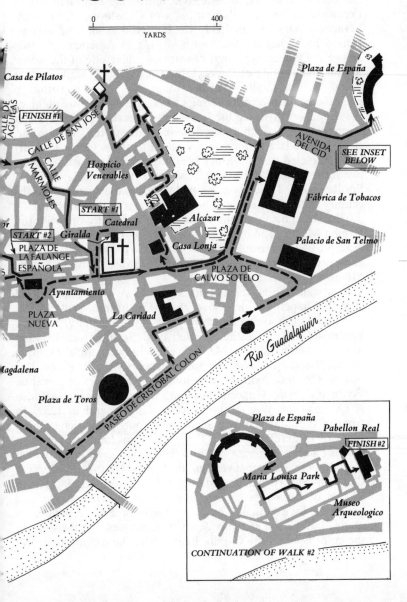

Seville

0   400
YARDS

Casa de Pilatos

CALLE DE AGUILAS

FINISH #1

CALLE DE SAN JOSÉ

CALLE DE SAN JOSÉ

CALLE MARMOLES

Hospicio Venerables

START #1
Catedral

START #2
Giralda

PLAZA DE LA FALANGE ESPAÑOLA

Alcázar

Casa Lonja

Ayuntamiento

PLAZA NUEVA

La Caridad

PLAZA DE CALVO SOTELO

Plaza de España

AVENIDA DEL CID

SEE INSET BELOW

Fábrica de Tobacos

Palacio de San Telmo

Magdalena

Plaza de Toros

PASEO DE CRISTOBAL COLON

Rio Guadalquivir

Plaza de España

Pabellon Real

FINISH #2

Maria Louisa Park

Museo Arqueologico

CONTINUATION OF WALK #2

Directly in front of you, about halfway to the enclosed area, in the floor of the central aisle, is a tombstone commemorating Fernando Colón or Columbus, son of Christopher Columbus. Fernando, who died in 1539, was himself a sailor, and accompanied his father on the fourth voyage to America, in 1502. Notice the faded engravings of ships on either side of the stone. Skirting the outside of the enclosed Coro (Choir), walk straight ahead to the **Capilla Mayor** (Main Chapel), set within a magnificent 16th-century wrought-iron grille. The highlight of the Capilla Mayor is the stupendous **retable** (altarpiece), a masterpiece of Gothic woodcarving, above the main altar. Begun in the late 15th century by the Flemish sculptor Dancart and completed half a century later, this retable consists of forty-five scenes from the lives of Christ, the Virgin, and the saints of Seville executed in carved, painted wood. In the center is a 14th-century statue, Virgen della Sede, patroness of the cathedral.

Turn around to visit the **Coro,** which is directly opposite the Capilla Mayor. The iron grille dates from 1519 and is another example of the versatile artistry of Dancart. The choirstalls are earlier, dating from about 1475, and are distinguished by the Moorish-style woodwork.

Now walk behind the Capilla Mayor to visit the **Capilla Real** (Royal Chapel). High above the wrought-iron grille is St. Ferdinand on horseback receiving the keys to the city. As King Ferdinand III of Castile, he delivered Seville from its long Moorish domination in 1248. This chapel is a beautiful example of the Plateresque style, the Renaissance style as it evolved in Spain. On the right is the tomb of Beatrice of Swabia, Ferdinand's wife. Opposite her tomb is that of her son, Alfonso X (Alfonso the Wise), who succeeded Ferdinand in 1252. In front of the altar stands a silver-and-bronze shrine containing the body of Ferdinand. Four times a year, his tomb is opened so that the public can view his reputedly undecayed body, which has lain here for over seven hundred years. On the altar itself is the 13th-century wooden statue called Virgen de los Reyes (Virgin of the Kings). There is a legend that this statue was presented to Ferdinand by King Louis of France, who also attained sainthood after his death. You can descend the steps to the crypt beneath the Capilla Real, where the coffins of several of Spain's rulers rest, including that of Pedro the Cruel, the mid-14th-century king who made Seville his capital and chief residence.

As you leave the Capilla Real, turn right to see the Capilla de San Pedro (St. Peter), with its **retable,** painted in 1625 by Francisco Zurbaran, illustrating the life of St. Peter in nine sections. Walk past the Capilla Real to the Capilla de la Purificación, in the southeast corner of the cathedral. From this small chapel you enter the **Sala Capitular,** the chapter house of the cathedral. This Plateresque room, built between 1530 and 1592, after the body of the cathedral was completed, contains a superb painting by Bartolomé Murillo entitled *The Immaculate Conception,* which hangs above the bishop's throne. Murillo, one of the most famous of Seville's native sons, also painted the series of ovals between the windows.

Next door is the entrance to the sacristy, another room in Plateresque style. Besides noting the numerous paintings by many well-known names, be sure to see (you can hardly miss them) the huge 16th-century monstrance in the form of a circular temple, the work of Juan de Arfe, and the tremendous twenty-two-foot-high bronze candelabrum executed in the mid-16th century by Bartolomé Morel and Pedro Delgado.

Walk along the south side of the cathedral to see the wealth of stained glass windows, products of the 16th through 19th centuries. Look for the Capilla de Nuestra Señora de los Dolores to the left of the south door. This chapel serves as the entrance to the **Sacristia de Calices** (Sacristy of the Chalices), with its treasury of paintings by several great Spanish artists, including Murillo, Zurbaran, Morales, Goya, and Juan de Valdes Leal, another Sevillan artist. On the altar is the early-17th-century sculpture of the Crucifixion by Martinez Montañes.

Just beyond the Capilla de los Dolores, next to the south door, is **Christopher Columbus's monumental mausoleum.** The sarcophagus of the discoverer of the New World is borne by four bronze figures representing the separate kingdoms of Spain—Castile, Aragon, Leon, and Navarre—before they were unified through the marriage of Ferdinand II of Aragon and Isabella of Castile. Columbus, who died in 1506, at the age of sixty, was first buried in San Domingo, Haiti, and then moved to the Cathedral in Havana, Cuba. He was returned to Seville in 1899, which is fitting since it was from the nearby town of Palos that Columbus sailed on his first journey to the New World, on August 3, 1492. Note the colossal fresco of St. Christopher to the left of the south door.

Continue along the south side of the cathedral to the Puerta del Nacimiento, the door to the left of the main entrance. Just to the left of this door is the altar of the Nativity with a splendid **retable,** *Adoration of the Shepherds,* painted in 1555 by the primitive artist Luis de Vargas. Past the three doorways on this west side of the cathedral, in the northwest corner, is the grandiose entrance to the 17th-century baroque church, the **Sagrario,** which serves as the parish church for the people of the community.

Just to the left of the entrance to the Sagrario as you leave is the Chapel of the Baptism. Appropriately enough, it is the cathedral's baptistry, and contains two fine paintings by Murillo: *St. Anthony of Padua* and, above it, *Baptism of Christ.* Continue along the north side to the north door, which leads to the large, lovely **Patio de los Naranjos** (Courtyard of the Oranges), once the courtyard of the mosque which occupied the site of the present cathedral. Examine the eight-sided fountain used by the Moslems more than 800 years ago; its base may date back even further to the days when the Visigoths ruled Seville, 1,500 years ago. To your left is the Sagrario, which you just visited. Across the courtyard is the battlemented wall with the Plateresque Puerta del Perdon (Gate of Pardon) in the center. The bronze plaques on this door are Arabic work of the 12th century, another reminder of the mosque which once existed here. To the right is the **Biblioteca Colombina** (hours: 10:30–12:30, 4–6:30 in summer), the 16th-century library housing the 3,000 books and manuscripts given by Fernando Columbus to the cathedral. In front of the library is the pulpit used by many famous preachers of the past five centuries, including St. Vincent Ferrar.

Before leaving the courtyard through the door in the southeast corner of the patio, don't miss seeing the Puerta del Lagarto (Door of the Alligator), which takes its name from the stuffed alligator hanging in the passageway, supposedly the gift of an

Egyptian potentate to the mosque. To your right once you've left the patio is the **Giralda,** the magnificent 300-foot bell tower which has come to symbolize the city of Seville. The bottom three-quarters of the bell tower was originally built in the late 12th century by the Moorish Almohade sultan Yusuf II to serve as the minaret to the city's chief mosque. When the Christians tore down the mosque, they kept the minaret intact. In 1568, the Cordovan architect Hernan Ruiz completed the five-story Renaissance bell tower which caps the minaret. On top of it all stands the 13-foot-high statue of Faith, which turns with the slightest breeze. This statue has been nicknamed Giraldilla (weathervane), and it is she who lends her name to the entire tower. You can climb a sloping ramp 230 feet to the top of the minaret portion of the tower for a spectacular view over the city (hours: 11–1, 5–7 in summer; 11–1, 3–5 in winter).

The Giralda stands in the Plaza de la Virgen de los Reyes (Square of the Virgin of the Kings), and to the left is the **Palacio Arzobispal,** the 17th-century baroque Archbishop's Palace. From the Palacio, walk along the north side of the Patio de los Naranjos just outside the battlemented wall. Turn right and stroll along Avenida José Antonio Primo de Rivera. Directly in front of you is the **Ayuntamiento,** Seville's City Hall. Walk to the right into the Plaza de la Falange Española, once the site of both bullfights and autos-da-fé, to examine the elaborately decorated east façade of this building. If you have time, wander up the main staircase inside to look at some of the offices with their vaulted or wooden ceilings.

After leaving the Ayuntamiento, walk around the building to the west façade, facing the **Plaza Nueva** (New Square), Seville's most spacious square, planted with palm and orange trees. As you stroll to the center of the square to see the equestrian statue of St. Ferdinand, notice the lovely wrought-iron lamps on colored marble bases around the square.

Return to Plaza de la Falange Española and take the street which leads out of the square on the right, **Calle de las Sierpes** (Street of the Serpents), so called because of its length and narrowness. This most famous and liveliest of Seville's streets is reserved for pedestrians only, and is lined with shops, souvenir stands, and cafés. If you get a chance, return here in the early evening for the *paseo,* when the street is crowded with natives and tourists alike ambling along slowly. About one-quarter of the way down the Sierpes, make a left turn into Calle Jovellanos to see the late-17th-century ultra-baroque chapel of San José (St. Joseph).

Return to Las Sierpes and continue your stroll past interesting shops and shoppers. When you come to the square called Campaña, at the end of Las Sierpes, turn left. In a few steps you will reach **Plaza Duque de la Victoria,** where there is a bronze statue of one of Seville's most famous native sons, the 17th-century artist Diego Velazquez, many of whose masterpieces hang in the Prado Museum in Madrid.

The Calle de Alfonso XII runs along the left side of this square; follow it until you come to another square, **Plaza del Museo** (Square of the Museum), on your left. In the center is a bronze statue of another of Seville's native sons, the 17th-century artist Bartolomé Murillo. Across the square is the **Museo de Bellas Artes,** Seville's Museum of Fine Arts (hours: 10-2, 4-8 in summer; closed Monday, and Sunday afternoon). Housed in what was once a convent, this museum is the most important in Spain, after the Prado in Madrid, because of its large collection of the country's leading artists. The entrance courtyard of the museum is lined with some of the most lovely *azulejos* (brightly colored glazed tiles) dating from the 16th and 17th centuries. What was once the convent's church now houses a collection of paintings by Francisco Zurbaran and Bartolomé Murillo. The Zurbarans hang in the church's nave. Zurbaran lived in the first half of the 17th century—the great age of Sevillan art—and was one of the foremost painters of Spanish religious subjects. Be sure to see *The Crowning of St. Joseph, The Conference of St. Bruno and Pope Urban II,* and *The Deification of St. Thomas Aquinas* (in this painting, Emperor Charles V appears on the right and the artist himself stands slightly behind the Emperor). In the transepts and choir hang some of the best of Bartolomé Murillo's work, which provides a striking contrast to his contemporary Zurbaran in its emphasis on the romantic rather than the realistic. Note especially his *Adoration of the Shepherds, St. Thomas of Villanueva Distributing Alms* (regarded by the artist himself as his finest painting), and the painting of

Sts. Justa and Rufina, Seville's patron saints, holding the Giralda.

Around the cloisters on the ground floor are paintings of another important Spanish artist, Juan de Valdes Leal, another 17th-century native Sevillan and contemporary of Zurbaran and Murillo. See his St. John, the Virgin, and the three Marys searching for Christ. Before you leave this excellent museum, visit the collection of contemporary and modern Spanish art, especially interesting as a contrast to all the 17th-century masterpieces you've been seeing.

From the museum, turn right and make a right turn at the corner. At the end of Calle Miguel de Carvajal, turn left into Calle de Bailén and walk to the Calle de San Pablo. On the corner, to your right, is the early-18th-century baroque church of **La Magdalena.** This grandiose church with its Moorish-style minaret is considered by some to be the most beautiful in Seville, and by others to be the most gaudy. Step inside to see the frescoes of Lucas Valdes, painted in the early 18th century.

Continue past La Magdalena along Calle de San Pablo, which soon becomes Calle de los Reyes Catolicos. At the end of this street, turn left and stroll along the Paseo de Cristobal Colón, which runs alongside Seville's river, the Guadalquivir. Across the river is the suburb of Triana, noted for its tile factories. On your left, you will soon pass Seville's bullring, **Plaza de Toros,** built in 1760 in Mudejar style, a blending of Moorish and either Romanesque or Gothic architectural styles. This bullring, one of the oldest and loveliest in Spain, is capable of seating fourteen thousand spectators. From March to October there are frequent bullfights staged here, and you should try to attend at least one.

A short distance past the bullring, turn left on Calle del Dos de Mayo and then right on Calle Temprado. On the left side of the street is **La Caridad** (Charity), a combination almshouse and hospital built in the mid-17th century by Miguel de Mañara. Mañara is supposed to have been the legendary Don Juan Tenorio, immortalized by countless writers and composers as Spain's great lover. Although the fictional Don Juan died unrepentant, the real Miguel de Mañara is supposed to have recognized the wickedness of his reckless ways. He joined the order of Caridad, which had as its prime function the burial of executed criminals, established the hospital you see before you today, and died here in 1679.

The façade is adorned with five large blue-and-white *azulejos,* which are attributed to Murillo. The entrance is at No. 3, and within the colonnaded courtyard is the baroque church. Just to the right of the west door is the famous realistic painting by Juan de Valdes Leal of two skeletons, one in knightly armor, the other in the robes of an archbishop. To the left of the same door is another Valdes Leal painting, *Triumph of Death.* On either side of the nave hang Murillo paintings, and Pedro Roldan's masterpiece, *Burial of Christ,* stands on the high altar. By the west door is the tomb of Miguel de Mañara with the inscription: HERE LIE THE DUST AND BONES OF THE WORST MAN WHO EVER LIVED.

Across from the entrance as you leave stands Miguel himself. Turn left and walk to Calle de Santander. Then turn right, and once again walk toward the river. Make a left, and across the street is another of Seville's landmarks, **Torre del Oro** (Tower of Gold), so named because it was believed to have been covered with gilded tiles at one time. Built in 1220 by the last Moorish rulers of Seville, just twenty-eight years before Ferdinand conquered the city, it served as a fortified defense on the river. It was connected to the Alcázar, the palace of the Moors, by an underground passage. In subsequent years, the Tower became a treasure house, then a prison, and today it houses a small Naval Museum (hours: Tuesday to Saturday, 10–2; Sunday, 10–1; closed Monday). The cupola was added in the 18th century.

Continue strolling along the Paseo, past the bridge crossing the Guadalquivir, until you come to the Avenida de Roma. Turn left; on the right is the massive baroque **Palacio de San Telmo,** originally a naval college in the 18th century. In 1849 it became the property of the son of the French king, Louis Philippe; now it is a seminary. Be sure to examine the fine main doorway, which was completed in 1734 and imitates the elaborate baroque architecture of José Churriguera. Step inside to see the beautiful courtyard.

When you come to the Plaza de Calvo Sotelo, with its lovely fountain, make a short detour to the right along Calle de San Fernando. You pass one of Seville's finest hotels on the right before coming to the huge baroque structure which once housed the city's **Fábrica de Tabacos** (tobacco factory). It is hard to imagine this grandiose building as a factory of any sort. Built in 1757, this is the largest building of historic interest in Spain after the monastery of El Escorial. At one time, ten thousand workers were employed here. You can almost visualize Bizet's Carmen lounging beside the main doorway. Today the building houses divisions of the city's university.

Return to Plaza Calvo Sotelo and walk toward the cathedral along Avenida Queipo de Llano. On the right, after a few steps, you will reach the entrance to **Casa Lonja** (Exchange House). This building was designed by Juan de Herrera, the architect of both El Escorial and the cathedral at Valladolid. In the late 16th century it was built to house the city's merchants, who up to that time had used the Patio de los Naranjos as their meetingplace. Climb the staircase leading to the **Archivo de Indias** (Archives of the Indies) (hours: 10–1), a collection of some thirty thousand documents relating to the Americas. Here you can examine the autographs of many famous explorers, including Columbus, Magellan, Pizarro, Cortez, Vespucci, and Balboa. Surprisingly enough, there is even a letter, dated 1789, from George Washington to the chiefs of the Choctaw tribe, concerning a treaty.

From Casa Lonja, turn left, then left again into the Plaza del Triunfo. Across the Plaza is the massive façade of another of Seville's landmarks, the **Alcázar.** Originally built in the late 12th–early 13th century, at about the same time the Giralda and the Torre del Oro were constructed, the Alcázar was both palace and fortress for the Moorish sultans who ruled the city. There are very few fragments of the building which existed then. The oldest parts today date back to the mid-14th-century reign of Pedro the Cruel. In the following century, Ferdinand and Isabella and, later, their grandson Emperor Charles V restored and enlarged both palace and gardens.

You enter the Alcázar (hours: 9–12:45, 4–6:30 in summer; Sunday, 9–12:45 only) through the Puerta del Leon (Door of the Lion), with its glazed-tile lion. This leads to the Patio del Leon, from which there is a good view of the mid-14th-century Mudejar façade erected by Pedro the Cruel. From this patio, you can enter the main portion of the Alcázar via the Puerta Principal. Proceed to the loveliest courtyard in the Alcázar, the **Patio de las Doncellas** (Courtyard of the Maidens). It is surrounded by a beautiful arcade of arches borne on twin marble columns, with a wealth of delicate arabesque tracery above the columns. Beneath the arcade, be sure to see the *artesonado* ceiling (of decorated, coffered wood), the exquisite Moorish doorways, and the medieval *azulejos* along the lower portion of the walls.

On the left side of the Patio, you enter the **Salon de Carlos V,** with its *azulejo* decoration and fine Mudejar *artesonado* ceiling, both dating from the 16th century. To the left of this salon is the **Salon de Embajadores** (Room of the Ambassadors), the most splendid room in the Alcázar. This salon is distinguished for its domed *artesonado* ceiling and its elaborately decorated walls, arches, and doorways. Note the portraits of Spanish kings and queens high up beneath the dome. Close by is another lovely courtyard, the **Patio de las Muñecas** (Courtyard of the Dolls), which takes its name from two small faces in its decoration, across from where you entered. These faces are very small and difficult to find, but they are almost unique. It is extremely unusual to have faces represented in Arabic art, and these were probably added by Christian workers employed by the Arabs.

After you've visited the various apartments, find time to stroll about the Alcázar's lovely **gardens,** with their fountains, ornamental ponds, and palm and orange trees. Stop at the mid-16th-century pavilion erected by Emperor Charles V, with its lovely *azulejos* and cedar dome. Leave the gardens through the Apeadero, an open hall of marble columns which leads to the Patio de Banderas, adjoining the Alcázar on its east end.

You are just outside the area of the city called **Santa Cruz,** one of the most picturesque quarters of Seville. This section of narrow, winding streets and alleys is lined with silent white houses with grilled windows and flowering balconies. It was once the Juderia, or Jewish ghetto, of the city. As you slowly stroll along, catch glimpses of the colorful patios behind the doors facing the street. From the Patio de Banderas, take the narrow street, Calle Juderia, left of the Patio. In a few feet, make a left turn into Calle Vida (Street of Life), which leads to the quiet **Plaza de Doña Elvira.** You might want to rest here a moment under the shady trees beside the fountain. Later on, you may feel like returning to hire a horse-drawn cab for a leisurely ride through some parts of the city you've already seen on foot.

Take the street leading out of the Plaza on the right, Calle Gloria (Street of Paradise). In the tiny Plaza de los Venerables stands the **Hospicio de los Venerables,** a 17th-century almshouse. Visit the baroque church (hours: 10–2, 5–9). It was completed in 1675, and the frescoes inside were painted by Juan de Valdes Leal. Here also you can see the **Museo de la Semana Santa** (Holy Week Museum), which displays some of the statues and costumes carried and worn during the elaborate ceremonies preceding Easter Sunday when the entire city seems to become one long ornate processional.

From the church, walk straight ahead along Calle Justino de Neve to **Callejon de Aqua** (Street of Water), one of the many interesting streets in this quarter. As you walk past the mansions, see if you can catch a glimpse of the lovely patios inside. Turn left along Callejon de Aqua, and in a few steps you are in Plaza Alfaro. The artist Murillo died in 1682 in the house at No. 2. Walk across the square and take the street in the upper left corner. This will lead you to **Plaza de Santa Cruz,** with its exquisite 17th-century wrought-iron cross, so delicate it looks like filigree. A synagogue once occupied this square, and Bartolomé Murillo lived at No. 10.

Walk to your left through the square and then along **Calle Santa Teresa,** which leads to Calle Ximenez de Enciso. Turn right and walk to Calle Santa Maria La Blanca (St. Mary the Pure Street). A few steps to your right takes you to the church of **Santa Maria La Blanca.** Until 1391, this church was a synagogue serving the Juderia. It was rebuilt as a baroque church in the mid-17th century. Go inside briefly to see Luis de Vargas's altarpiece above the main altar.

From Santa Maria, turn right and continue along Calle Santa Maria La Blanca, which becomes Calle de San José. To your right you pass the lovely gold-and-white church of San José. Now continue on until you come to what was formerly the Convento de la Madre de Dios (Convent of the Mother of God). These buildings are now occupied by the medical school of the university. The convent's church was built in the mid-16th century. Go inside to see its fine *artesonado* ceiling and the effigies of the wife and daughter of Mexico's conqueror, Hernan Cortez.

If you still have enough energy left, you might want to continue walking around this fascinating and colorful quarter, discovering on your own some particularly picturesque corner. You are only about five or ten minutes away from the cathedral.

Your second walking tour through Seville will take you to many of the city's lovely churches and mansions. Although it's a lengthy walk, you will get the chance to see many of the city's different streets and avenues and to pass through a variety of neighborhoods. As the highlight of the day, you will end your walk in Seville's loveliest park.

Begin your walk in the Plaza de la Falange Española, just in front of the City Hall. Walk toward Calle de las Sierpes, but take the street which runs to the right and leads to the Plaza del Salvador (Square of Our Savior). Dominating the square is Seville's second largest church, **El Salvador,** considered one of the foremost examples of the baroque style in Seville. Built on the site of the city's first grand mosque, the church still retains parts of that structure. Inside are two masterpieces of statuary, Juan de Mesa's *Cristo del Amor (Christ of Love)* and Martinez Montañes's *Jesus de la Pasion (Jesus of the Passion),* both sculpted in the early 17th century, and both still proudly carried through the city in procession during Holy Week.

From the church, turn right into Calle de Cuna. At No. 8 you come to the **Palacio de la Condesa de Lebrija** (Palace of the Countess of Lebrija), a lovely Renaissance-style mansion. Inside is an interesting collection of mosaics, many of them from the former city of Italica, five miles outside Seville. Founded in 200 B.C., Italica was once a thriving city. The Roman emperors Trajan and Hadrian were both natives of this city, and it boasted an amphitheater which could seat forty thousand spectators, thermal baths, and luxurious villas. Italica met its end in the 8th century, when the Moors overran and destroyed it. Today you can visit its ruins or see a portion of its treasures here in this

Renaissance palace. You must ask the porter for admission, since this is a private museum. A better idea is to ask your hotel concierge to call in advance for you. A little farther along this same street, at No. 3, you will pass another of Seville's beautiful old mansions, Casa del Marques de la Montilla.

At the end of the Calle de Cuna, turn right along Calle Laraña. On the right side of this street, you come to the Antigua Universidad (Old University). Founded in 1502 by Archdeacon Roderigo, the university has occupied its present quarters, a Jesuit monastery of the 16th century, since 1771. Adjacent to the University is the **University Church.** On the right and left sides of the nave are the Renaissance tombs of two of Seville's nobility, Don Pedro Enriquez de Rivera and his wife, Doña Catalina. They are the parents of Don Fadrique, whose beautiful home, Casa de Pilatos, we shall visit later on. Above the high altar is the retable, with the painting of the Holy Family in the center, the work of the 17th-century naturalistic artist Juan de las Roelas. On either side of this painting are two statues by Montañes, of Sts. Francis Borgia and Ignatius Loyola.

From the university, return down Calle Laraña. Turn right to walk along Calle Orfila, which becomes Calle Daoiz. You pass the brightly colored church of San Andrés. If it's open, step inside for a moment to see the beautiful *azulejos* along the bottoms of the pillars. Turn left, and ahead is Calle del Amor de Dios (Street of the Love of God). Make a right turn. At the end of this street stretches the fine wide promenade called **Alameda de Hercules** (Avenue of Hercules), bordered by 16th-century houses and numerous cafés and bars. Directly in front of you are two immense granite pillars, which were moved to this site in 1574. They were once part of an ancient Roman temple which stood on the Calle Marmoles. Today these two pillars bear statues of Hercules and Julius Caesar.

Walk past the statues and turn left until you come to the Calle Conde de Barajas. Turn right and stroll to the Plaza San Lorenzo, a secluded oasis lined with houses with colorful patios. Here stands the church of **San Lorenzo** (St. Lawrence). The mosque which once stood in this spot was replaced by a Gothic-style church which was largely rebuilt in the 17th century. Notice the two lovely *azulejos* on either side of the door, and the retable of the high altar, the work of Montañes. To the left of San Lorenzo is a small building called **Templo del Gran Poder** (Temple of Great Power), with a masterpiece of the 17th-century sculptor Juan de Mesa on the altar.

At the west end of the square, turn right to walk along Calle de Santa Clara Esclava. At the corner of Calle de Santa Ana and Calle de Santa Clara you pass the large church of Santa Ana. Just beyond, at No. 23, on the opposite side of the street, is the 17th-century Palacio de Santa Coloma. At No. 42 is a gateway leading to the 13th-century **Convento de Santa Clara.** The convent's Renaissance church has a splendid *artesonado* ceiling, as well as statuary by Montañes. Especially note his St. Francis of Assisi. The retable of the high altar is also the work of Montañes and his pupils, and was executed between 1621 and 1623.

To the right of the church as you leave is the **Torre de Don Fadrique** (hours: 9–2, 3–6), a unique 13th-century tower in transitional Romanesque-Gothic style. This tall battlemented tower was once part of the no-longer-existent palace of Don Fadrique, brother of the 13th-century King Alfonso X.

Continue along Calle Santa Clara to the **Monastery of San Clemente** (No. 92), founded by the saint king, Ferdinand III, in the 13th century on the site of a Moorish palace. The structure you see today dates back to 1632, although many elements, such as the *artesonado* ceiling and the *azulejos,* belong to the earlier church established by Ferdinand. Inside, be sure to notice Juan de Valdes Leal's frescoes.

From the church, turn left, then left again on Calle del Reposo. Cross the street into Pasaje del Conde de Mejorada, which leads to Calle de Becquer, named in honor of the Spanish Romantic poet Gustavo Adolfo Becquer. Turn right and walk several blocks to the **Puerta de la Macarena** (Gateway of the Macarena) on your left. This ancient gate, named for a Moslem princess, is part of the old town wall first erected by the Romans, then restored by the Moors in the 11th and 12th centuries and finally rebuilt in the 18th century. You can still see a considerable remnant of the wall with its towers and battlements to the left of the Puerta de la Macarena.

The long street Calle de San Luis begins at the Puerta. To the right just beyond the gateway is the **Basilica de la Macarena** (hours: 9–1, 5–9). It contains Seville's most famous and best-loved statue, *La Macarena,* patroness of bullfighters, and is the work of the 17th-century sculptor Pedro Roldan. During Holy Week the statue is carried in procession through the city, adorned in splendid robes and ornamented with precious jewels lent by the wealthy women of the community. Nearby is a museum where the statue's accessories and ornaments are stored until Eastertime. You can also see the regalia worn by Manolete, one of Spain's most famous bullfighters, who was killed in the ring in 1947. Also here is an example of one of the pasos or floats carried through the city during Holy Week on the backs of parishioners.

Leave the basilica and continue along Calle de San Luis. After a stroll of about five minutes, you will pass the church of **Santa Marina** on your left, with its 14th-century Mudejar tower erected on an even earlier Moorish base. Across the street is the circular church of **San Luis,** built 250 years ago in ornate baroque style.

Once again resume your walk along Calle de San Luis. On your left, you will pass the 14th-century church of **San Marcos,** with its unusual 14th-century Mudejar portal and 17th-century statues. The base of the church's bell tower was the minaret for the mosque which once stood here. In the mid-14th century, the Mudejar tower was erected on the Moorish base. Although this tower is no competition for the Giralda, it rises seventy-five feet and is the second highest in the city. The interior of this church looks more like a mosque than any other church you've seen so far. Its starkness is a pleasant contrast to the gold and glitter of the others.

Along the south side of San Marcos runs the Calle de Santa Paula. On the left you pass the church of Santa Isabel, a simple façade with an elegant classical doorway. Follow this street to the **Convento de Santa Paula,** which was founded in 1475. The convent's church has a 16th-century Mudejar doorway adorned with polychrome *azulejos.* On the tympanum over the door are the combined coats of arms of the provinces of Aragon and Castile whose foremost representatives were Ferdinand and Isabella. Inside are a rich Mudejar ceiling, 16th-century *azulejos* on the walls, late Gothic tombs, and several works by Montañes, including his *John the Baptist* carved in 1638.

Return to Calle de San Luis and take the second left, Calle de Bustos Tavera. After one block, take the street to the right, the narrow, curving Calle Doña Maria Coronel. After about three hundred feet you will come to the Calle de las Dueñas (Street of the Chaperones) on the right, where you will see the **Casa de las Dueñas** at No. 5. This is the impressive 15th-century mansion of the Dukes of Alba, one of Spain's most noble families (hours: 11–1, 4:30–6:30). Go inside to see the Plateresque patio, the Gothic chapel adorned with *azulejos,* and the lovely rooms decorated in the style of the 15th to 17th centuries.

Return to Calle Doña Maria Coronel and continue along for one short block to Calle de Gerona. Turn left, and soon you will see the church of **Santa Catalina** (St. Catherine) sitting at the crossroads of several busy streets. Formerly a mosque, this church has retained an ancient minaret. Step inside to see the Moorish chapel off the south aisle, with its beautiful *artesonado* ceiling. To the left of the high altar is the highly ornate baroque chapel in the style of the 18th-century architect José Churriguera, quite a contrast to the simplicity of the nave.

From the main entrance to Santa Catalina take the Calle Almirante Apodaca, which leads to the Plaza Argüelles. Here stands the church of **San Pedro,** a Gothic structure which was rebuilt in the 17th century. Its most distinguishing characteristic is its Mudejar bell tower. The artist Diego de Velazquez was baptized in this church in 1599.

The Calle Descalzos runs out of the southeast end of the Plaza Argüelles. You pass the grand-looking façade of San Ildefonso, and Calle Descalzos becomes Calle Caballerizas (Street of Stables). Follow this street to the **Casa de Pilatos** (House of Pilate), the residence of the present Dukes of Medinaceli, and the finest mansion in Seville. Casa de Pilatos was begun about the year 1480 by Don Pedro Enriquez de Rivera, whose tomb you saw earlier in the church of the Old University. His son, Fadrique, the first Marquis of Tarifa and ancestor of the present Duke, completed the mansion in the early 16th century. The house received its name because Don Fadrique made a pilgrimage to the Holy Land in 1519 and returned determined to build his home in the style of Pontius Pilate's residence in Jerusalem. Despite Fadrique's intentions, the house is much more Mudejar and Plateresque than Roman.

The interior is splendid (hours: 9–1, 4–7 in summer). The patio is surrounded by arcades supported on white marble columns and decorated with *azulejos*. In the center is a marble fountain with dolphins at its base and a bust of Janus, the two-faced god, above the basin. In the corners of the patio stand four large marble statues from the ruined city of Italica. To the right of the patio is a room called the Praetorium, one of the finest examples of the Plateresque style in Seville. Don't miss the fine *artesonado* ceiling.

The Casa de Pilatos sits at the edge of the Plaza de Pilatos, with its statue of the 17th-century artist Zurbaran. Just a few steps east of the Plaza is the 14th-century church of **San Estaban** (St. Stephen). Another 17th-century artist, Juan de Valdes Leal, was baptized in this church in 1622.

Return to Plaza de Pilatos and follow the Calle de Aguilas (Street of the Eagles), which leads out of the square on the left. Turn left on Calle Cabeza del Rey Don Pedro. Where the street divides, take the left fork, Calle Muñoz y Pabón. Look to the right for the tiny, narrow Calle Marmoles (Marble Street) which gives you a strong indication of what we're looking for here. You will see to your right three immense gray granite columns, each thirty feet tall, remnants of an ancient Roman temple which stood here two thousand years ago. Additional columns were moved to the Alameda de Hercules four centuries ago; you saw them earlier in this walk.

After all this church and mansion touring, it's time for a visit to the park, and Seville has a lovely one, the Maria Luisa. Since it's a mile away, you might want to hail a cab and ask to be dropped off at Plaza de España. If you decide to walk, take the Calle del Aire and turn left on Calle de los Abades. Turn right when you reach Calle de Segovias. This street runs into Calle de Argote de Molina, and you'll soon see the Giralda to your left. Walk along the cathedral's north side to Avenida Queipo de Llano. Turn left and walk to Plaza Calvo Sotelo, then up Calle de San Fernando and past the former Tobacco Factory to Glorietta de Don Juan de Austria. Turn right along Avenida del

Cid to Glorietta de San Diego. Cross this circular "square" and bear left along Avenida de Isabel la Catolica. On your right is Maria Luisa Park, and to your left is the **Plaza de España,** a magnificent semicircular plaza bounded by a vast government building with colorful *azulejos.* In front of the building is a semicircular canal crossed by tiled bridges. Stroll around the area to admire the benches, one for each important Spanish city, decorated with lively colored *azulejos* depicting an event connected with each city.

Cross the street and enter the park. The **Maria Luisa** is Seville's loveliest park with its multitude of fountains and statues, colorful *azulejo* benches to sit on and watch passersby, cafés, flowers, and palm and orange trees. If you're tired, it's the perfect spot to rest and regain your energy. If you've got energy to spare, there's plenty to see here. In 1929, the Spanish-American Exhibition was held in Seville, and many of the buildings erected then are still here in the Maria Luisa. If you turn left and walk toward the south end of the park, you will see the Mudejar-style **Pabellon Real** (Royal Pavilion). Across from the Pavilion is the palace erected for the 1929 exhibition, now the home of the city's archeological museum, **Museo Arqueologico** (hours: 9-2, 4-6; closed Monday). The museum contains fine statuary from the Iberian, Greek, and Roman periods of Seville's early history, including remnants of the ruined city of Italica. Opposite this museum is one which houses paintings and costumes. It seems particularly appropriate to end your walk through this vital city among the reminders of its past.

INDEX

All things change—including walking-tour directions and sights. If you encounter any permanent changes during your walks, we would very much appreciate your letting us know about them.

CITY

DATE OF VISIT

COMMENT

YOUR NAME AND ADDRESS (optional)

MAIL TO: Juliann Skurdenis & Lawrence Smircich
More Walk Straight Through the Square
c/o David McKay Company, Inc.
750 Third Avenue
New York, New York 10017

THANK YOU!